The Curry
Book

The Curry Book

by

**Laxmi Khurana, Asha Naran
and Shelina Jetha**

Contents

Introduction

Indian curries, and spicy dishes in general, have become common and increasingly popular outside India over the past few years. This book explains how Indian cooking can be simple, based on a few, well-known spices which are easily available.

Starters and meat curry dishes are pretty standard, and easily understood by most people. However, the dhals and vegetable curries offer a lot of variety and are much used in Indian homes, but are not readily available in restaurants. Therefore, besides covering the more popular meat and sundry cookery, this book covers a range of dhal and vegetable dishes to give you the opportunity of trying them.

Curry is a name given to a dish made using turmeric, chilli powder and other spices. Contrary to popular belief it does not necessarily have to have a thick spicy sauce. You will find several recipes in this book which have hardly any sauce and then there are other recipes which are really quite dry. With dishes like that it is a good idea to serve a yoghurt-based raita or a pulse dish.

Utensils and Equipment
There are some basic utensils and equipment needed for Indian cooking. A tavi – a heavy-based, flat, iron pan which is round and slightly concave – can be bought at most Indian shops and will be useful if you want to make chapattis. If you are buying one, make sure it has a handle! A pair of tongs will also be needed if you are new to chapatti making. If a tavi is not available then a large, heavy-based, non-stick frying pan will do just as well.

Also useful are a liquidiser or food processor; a sieve or skimmer (used for deep frying foods); a wok, or a large, deep frying pan; a pressure cooker; a colander; and a large serving spoon (the sort with spoon measurements marked on it).

Some recipes, such as Sev, require the use of a special snack-making device which consists of a wide metal tube with a handle on one side and five or six discs which fit at the other end.

A herb mill is very useful for chopping small amounts of ginger, garlic or green chillies. It also means you can avoid handling the green chillies which cause a burning sensation that can easily be transferred to other parts of the body. If you do have to chop your chillies by hand, make sure you wash your hands properly afterwards.

In India, and in many restaurants in the UK, a tandoor is often used. The tandoor is a clay oven, which is heated to a very high temperature in excess of 430°C (800°F). Most Indian homes in the UK do not have a tandoor, and therefore normally use an ordinary oven for tandoori dishes.

Preparation and Cooking Times

The preparation and cooking times given for some of the recipes are quite long – several hours in a few instances. Of course this does not mean that you will be kept busy for hours just to make the one meal! The preparation and cooking times include the periods during which the ingredients are soaking or marinating – an important procedure which imparts the characteristic flavour to many Indian recipes. But these times do indicate to the busy cook whether a particular recipe can be ready for supper tonight!

Please bear in mind that since all cooks work at different speeds, the preparation and cooking time included in each recipe can only give an approximate indication of the time taken to prepare the dish; it is not an exact timing!

Methods

Marinating

In Indian cooking, the process of marinating is frequently used to flavour foods. Marinating is often done by soaking the food to be flavoured in a mixture of yoghurt and spices. The minimum amount of time for marinating is about four hours, but the longer you leave food marinating, the better it tastes. This is especially true of tandoori dishes, where the fresh meat needs to marinate for about eight to twelve hours. Marination also serves to tenderise meat.

8

Frying and Deep Frying

For best results when frying, use vegetable oil.

Where 'deep frying' is required, make sure that the pan is at least half to three quarters full of oil. The ingredients to be deep fried should be almost submerged in the oil. You can tell if the oil is hot enough by testing a small amount of the ingredients to be fried. Any oil that is used for deep frying need not be discarded after use, but can be re-used for making the saks which are spicy or curried vegetable dishes with little or no sauce. Doing this will, in fact, add more flavour to these dishes!

In some of the recipes (such as Meat Biryani and Kalio), deep fried, golden brown onions are required. The onions should be peeled, chopped and fried in hot oil. Make sure you use a deep pan and be careful that the onions do not cause the oil to froth and spill over. To prevent this, only fry a handful at a time. The onions should look as if they are nearly burnt (a dark golden brown colour) and be crispy when cool.

Dry Cooking

In some recipes (such as Beef Samosas and Bateta Chops), it is suggested in the method that you 'dry cook' the meat. This means that the meat is cooked without any oil or other liquid. The meat should be cooked on a high heat and stirred frequently until it turns brown. The fat in the meat itself aids the process of cooking and for these recipes the final mixture needs to be as dry as possible, which is why no liquid is added.

Ingredients

Quantities of Ingredients

Indian cooking is an acquired art. You can never be very precise about the quantity of spices; it depends very much on your own taste. Sometimes it is worth experimenting with quantities until you arrive at the blend which suits your own taste buds. It is always best to start with a minimum of spices, as in this book. After a while, perhaps you might like to add other spices to the recipes in very small quantities, to experiment with flavours. You should not be afraid to do this, as all Indian cooking has been handed down through the generations, each generation varying the blends of spices in its own way. In most Indian households today, the same curry cooked on different days may well taste slightly different. The measurements of spices in this book should therefore be used more as basic guidelines, rather than as hard and fast rules.

Both metric and imperial measurements are given in this book. However, you should use only one set of measurements when following a recipe since exact equivalents are not given.

Spices

When you add the whole spices needed to give recipes the right flavours – such as cardamom pods, cinnamon sticks, bay leaves, cloves, peppercorns and chillies – they will not disintegrate during cooking, so warn your guests to look out for these when eating such dishes. The whole spices can be eaten by those who are accustomed to their hotness, or set aside by those who are unaccustomed (or unadventurous).

In proper Indian cooking (and in all the recipes here) curry powder is always added to a recipe in the early stages of cooking. This means that it is cooked properly, killing any salmonella bacteria that may be contained in it. Make sure that you do the same, and don't be tempted to sprinkle uncooked powder onto your food after cooking.

Almonds

A number of recipes for sweet dishes use almonds which will need peeling. The quickest way to do this is to steep them in hot water for 10 minutes. This loosens the skins and makes it easier to peel them.

Chillies and Mustard Seeds

Care must be taken when handling 'hot' spicy ingredients like chillies and chilli powder. Always wash your hands thoroughly after handling hot spices or spicy ingredients because they can cause a very nasty burning sensation on the skin which is easily transferred from the hands to other parts of the body.

Fresh chillies can be used with or without the seeds. If you want the hotness from the chillies then include the seeds but leave them out if all you require is a gentle flavouring. The chillies used can be either red or green, but should be of the 'hot' variety.

Several of the recipes start with the 'popping' of certain spices in hot oil. This technique is called 'vaghar'. Watch out when adding mustard seeds to hot oil – they will pop like crazy! Make sure that the heat is turned down, or better still, take the pan off the heat to control the temperature of the oil and then add the mustard seeds before returning to the heat.

Care should be taken to cover the pan with its lid while the spices are 'popping'. It is safer to take the pan off the heat when adding the vegetables or pulses to the hot oil as it is likely to splatter.

Sugar and Milk
Where the use of sugar is suggested, such as in the syrup for Jardo and Gulab Jamboos, it is best to use granulated white sugar. Also, be warned: melted sugar is very hot, so be careful not to splash yourself!

In some of the recipes such as that for Kheer, use whole pasteurised, full-fat milk for the best results.

Vegetables
In some regions of India many of the inhabitants are vegetarian, and therefore vegetables play an important part in their diets. Over the years they have devised hundreds of ways of cooking them, some with no sauce at all, some with just a hint of sauce and some in which the vegetables are literally swimming in a thick aromatic sauce.

There is a tremendous variety of vegetable dishes in Indian cooking. Most of the vegetables, such as potatoes, peas, aubergines, okra and peppers, are sold in English shops. The book does, however, include recipes which contain four rather uncommon vegetables. These are tindora, valor, kadu and guaer. These are available from most Indian shops, and obviously have to be bought fresh. They are well worth a try if you enjoy experimenting. The Indian names can be used to buy them and more information on them is given in the Glossary.

Pulses
Pulses, called dhals, are different types of seeds, used to make a variety of dishes. There are about fifteen different types of dhals; and these can be bought in bulk and stored for up to a year. It is very difficult to describe all the different types of seeds in English; only a couple are well-known in English households, namely lentils and chick peas. Most other varieties are available in Indian shops, and the Indian names may be used to buy them (see pages 278-288). Dhals are an acquired taste, and there is a tremendous variety in the way they can be cooked and, accordingly, in their flavour. They are usually served with rice, or another curry. Care must be taken in cooking dhals, to ensure that the seeds are well-boiled. They should not be eaten raw. This is because, unless cooked properly, they can be difficult to digest. In all the dhal recipes, cooking times should be carefully adhered to.

Different types of dhals are often ground to make flour. This flour is used to make poppadums, dhokra and a variety of other dishes. Also used in Indian cooking are two very commonly used flours: besan, or gram, flour, and chapatti flour. Besan flour is made from ground black grams, which are pulses. Chapatti flour is made from ground wheat. Neither of these flours has a direct English equivalent, but both are easily obtainable from Indian shops, or healthfood stores.

Dhals often contain impurities like dust particles and chaff. So before they are cooked, they need to be washed properly. This is done in one of two ways. The seeds can be individually sorted out, a few at a time and the impurities individually picked out. This method is the best, but is very laborious and time-consuming.

A faster method which is nearly as successful is to wash the dhal in such a way that the impurities sink to the bottom or float to the top. This is done by taking two large pans and placing the dhal in one of them. Add plenty of cold water so that it covers the dhal by about 5cm (2 in). Now shake the pan so as to stir the dhal. The chaff floats to the top and can be thrown away. Transfer the rest of the contents gradually to the second pan until very little dhal is left in the first pan. The impurities should be at the bottom with this small amount of dhal. This residue can either be discarded with the impurities or carefully picked so that all the impurities are thrown away. Repeat this process of mixing fresh water, stirring and transferring the contents back and forth about six to seven times. This method has something in common with the principles of 'gold panning' in olden times.

Grains

In Indian culinary history, rice dates back to as early as 2800 BC. It is eaten throughout the country and is prepared in various different ways. Biriyani and pilau must be the two most popular ways of serving rice. While plain boiled rice is perhaps more commonly eaten in most Indian homes, pilaus and biriyanies are usually cooked for special occasions and dinner parties.

Grains such as rice, lentils, and mung beans are best cooked after pre-soaking them in water. Make sure the grains are completely immersed in the water and not floating freely. After soaking for the required period (as per the recipe), drain off the water and use fresh water for the cooking process. The grains should be added to cold water and then brought to the boil. Allow to simmer until the grains have cooked (they will be tender to the touch).

If you use the dry grains of kidney beans, make sure you pre-soak them at least overnight and boil thoroughly before adding to the recipe (for at least 40 minutes, until just soft and mushy). Alternatively you can use tinned, pre-cooked kidney beans if you prefer.

Serving the Meal

As a final note, you may be interested to know how a typical Indian meal would be served. Usually, it would start with drinks, and an assortment of savoury snacks, whilst sitting around before dinner. Many of these snack dishes may be used as starters at dinner parties. More substantial dishes can even be served as the main course.

Once at the table, the meal typically begins with sweet or savoury starters. Spicy vegetable or meat dishes and breads are served with a sweet dish as the first course of a meal, followed by one or two meat dishes, accompanied by a rice dish with one vegetable curry and/or dhal. Chapattis or parathas or puris are also served at the same time, but usually only one of the options is served. An Indian would never dream of serving curries with anything but some freshly cooked Indian bread of one sort or another.

Raitas, poppadums and a variety of pickles and chutneys should also be placed on the table, together with a fresh salad. Normally, as the dishes are laid out, the diners help themselves to a selection of each as they require. Chutneys and pickles help tantalize taste buds and add a certain 'je ne sais quoi' to the meal. Raitas (yoghurt-based sauces), on the other hand, add a tang to the meal and some of them actually help to cool down a hot curry. The idea is to choose the appropriate pickle or raita for each meal.

In India, sweet dishes are served as part of the main meal. A dessert as such is often not served. Most people prefer to end their meal with fresh fruit. Indian sweet dishes tend to be quite rich in the use of milk and ghee so they should be served in small quantities. Little glass bowls are ideal for this.

Whether you would like to do what the Indians do or decide to have your sweet dish at the end of a meal, you are sure to enjoy the recipes in this section of the book.

Drinks to accompany Indian meals are usually non-alcoholic, as the spicy food tends to detract from the flavour of wine, and vice versa. Therefore, either iced water with a slice of lemon and a small amount of sugar is served, or lassi (yoghurt and water combined). However, wine or beer can be served, according to individual taste.

13

The meal may be followed by coffee or tea. Indian tea is made by adding tea, a teaspoonful of fennel seeds and 2 or 3 cardamoms to water, bringing the water to the boil and boiling for about 3 to 4 minutes, adding milk and boiling again for about 2 to 3 minutes, thus making a strong brew of tea. This is usually served, accompanied on a plate by fennel seeds mixed with sugar crystals.

This should give you some guidelines, if you are planning on having a full Indian meal, on how to serve and what dishes to combine.

Indian cookery is fun and flexible. Practice makes perfect and the recipes are designed to give you guidelines. Once you feel confident . . . let your taste buds do the cooking.

So relax, enjoy the cooking and bon appétit!

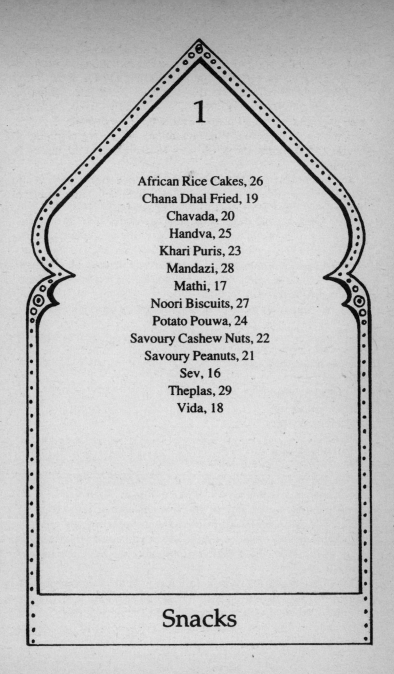

1

Snacks

SEV

Of all the dry snacks this crispy gram flour snack must be one of the most popular because it is very versatile: it can be eaten as it is on its own, it can be mixed with other dry snacks to make different combinations, or it can be used to sprinkle over soft snack dishes to give them a crunch. An example of this is Spicy Sweetcorn (page 46). Sev is also used, crushed, in certain dishes to thicken and flavour them.

For this recipe you will need a snack-making device. It consists of a wide metal tube with a handle on one side and five or six discs that fit at the other end. Each of the discs has a different size and shape of holes cut into it. The disc with tiny round holes is used for sev making. The metal tube is filled with the sev batter and the handle is turned to squeeze the batter out of the holes straight into hot oil. If your chilli powder is coarse it may be a good idea to grind it down first before using it in this recipe. This is just to stop it from clogging up the holes in the disc.

Sev will stay fresh in an airtight container for up to a month.

Cooking and preparation time: 30–35 minutes   *Serves:* several

225g (8 oz) gram flour
1 tsp salt
1 tsp chilli powder
1 tbsp cooking oil
1 tbsp lemon juice
tepid water
oil for deep frying

1. Sift the flour and salt into a bowl. Sprinkle on the chilli powder and mix with a spoon. Make a hole in the centre and add the oil and lemon juice and rub in. Now add enough tepid water to make a very thick batter. It should have a slow dropping consistency. Fit the snack-maker with the correct disc and fill with some of the batter. Screw back the lid tightly and you are ready to start frying.
2. Pour cooking oil into a wok until it is 5–6cm (2–2½ in) deep in the centre. Place it over a medium heat and heat until a small drop of batter, when dropped into the oil, starts to sizzle almost immediately. This will mean that the oil has reached the correct temperature.

3. Holding the snack-maker tightly over the hot oil, turn the handle. Move your hands in a clockwise direction as the thin strands of batter enter the hot oil. Stop turning the handle when you have made between 1½–2 full circles in the oil and break off the strands.
4. Now put down the snack-maker and, using two slotted spoons, turn over the sev in the oil. Cook for 10–15 seconds and then remove from the oil and drain on absorbent kitchen roll paper.
5. Sev should not be brown, so if your first batch is too brown you should reduce the heat slightly. If, on the other hand, it is still soft, you will need to turn up the heat before you cook your next batch. When all the sev is fried, allow to cool and then gently break up all the round nest shapes and pack in an airtight container. Use within one month.

MATHI

This is a savoury biscuit, made with plain flour, which is usually served with a cup of tea or coffee. It can also be used in packed lunches, picnics, or at parties. In fact it makes a good substitute for biscuits, especially if you like savoury snacks. Cooked mathis, like biscuits, can be stored in an airtight tin for up to six or seven weeks. For this recipe you need a wok or deep frying pan.

Cooking and preparation time: 2 hours   *Makes:* about 60 mathis

450g (1 lb) plain flour
85g (3 oz) butter or soft margarine
½ tsp salt
1 tsp ground black pepper
90ml (3 fl oz) water
1200ml (2 pt) cooking oil for frying

1. Sieve the plain flour into a large mixing bowl, and add the butter (or margarine), salt and ground pepper and mix well.
2. Mix in the water gradually until a medium soft dough is formed. (Make sure that you do not add too much water at a time.)

(continued overleaf)

3. Divide the mixture into little balls, about 4 cm (1½ in) in diameter.

4. Roll each ball into a circle about 7cm (3 in) in diameter and about 2mm (⅛ in) thick.

5. Make a couple of 2.5cm (1 in) marks on the rolled mathi, with a sharp knife. The knife should only penetrate the top and not cut through the whole thickness of the mathi.

6. Lay the rolled balls out separately.

7. Heat the oil in a wok or a deep frying pan to a high temperature. When it is hot, add about three mathis at a time and let them deep fry for a few seconds. Soon they will float to the top; now turn them and fry the mathis until they are golden brown all over. (The browning process on each mathi should take about 2 minutes; if it takes less time the oil is too hot and therefore the heat should be lowered.)

8. Let the mathis cool and then store them in an airtight tin.

VIDA

This is an unusual savoury snack made with cornflour. For this recipe you need a deep frying pan, or wok, and a liquidiser.

Cooking and preparation time: 12 hours 40 minutes   *Serves:* 4

225g (8 oz) cornflour
90ml (3 fl oz) yoghurt
120ml (4 fl oz) water
55g (2 oz) fresh garlic, peeled
55g (2 oz) fresh ginger, peeled
4 green chillies
½ tsp salt
½ tsp turmeric powder
½ tsp chilli powder
600ml (1 pt) cooking oil for frying

1. Sieve the cornflour into a bowl. Add the yoghurt and mix well. Add water gradually and continue to mix until a stiff dough is formed. Cover the bowl and leave for about 12 hours.

2. Process the garlic, ginger and chillies in a liquidiser until finely chopped.

3. Add the salt, turmeric powder, chilli powder and liquidiser contents into the stiff dough. Mix everything together. Take a small amount of dough at a time; shape it first into a ball and then pat the ball into a circle about 4cm (1½ in) in diameter and 0.5cm (¼ in) thick. Wet the palms of your hands with water occasionally while doing this. These shapes are called 'vidas.'

4. Heat the oil in a wok or deep frying pan to a high temperature, and fry the vidas (five to seven at a time) in the oil. Deep fry the vidas on a low heat. The frying process should take about 3–4 minutes; if it takes less then the oil is too hot. When the vidas are golden brown place them in a serving dish and serve while hot.

CHANA DHAL FRIED

This is a deep fried split chick pea dish, usually served with a cup of tea or coffee. It can also be munched while watching television or just relaxing. Fried chick peas can be stored in an airtight tin for four to five weeks and used as and when needed. For this recipe you need a wok or deep frying pan.

Cooking and preparation time: 12 hours *Makes:* about 900g (2 lb)

900g (2 lb) dried split peas
1200ml (2 pt) cooking oil for frying
1 tsp salt
1 tsp turmeric powder
1 tsp chilli powder

1. Soak the split peas in about 2 litres (3½ pt) of water overnight.

2. Drain all the water from the split peas, and spread the peas on some clean kitchen roll paper.

3. Heat the oil in a wok or deep frying pan to a high temperature. Add small amounts of the split peas to the oil and deep fry until they are golden brown. Another method of checking if they are ready is

(continued overleaf)

to eat one. It should feel hard and crunchy. Remove the fried split peas with a sieve and spread them on some fresh clean kitchen roll paper. Repeat with the remaining peas.

4. Add the salt, turmeric powder, and chilli powder to the peas and mix well. Transfer the contents to an airtight tin. This will keep the Chana Dhal Fried fresh for about a month.

CHAVADA

Chavada is a mixture of deep fried spiced nuts and seeds such as dried split chick peas, and is used as a savoury snack, usually served with a cup of tea or coffee. It can also be used in packed lunches, picnics or parties. Chavada can be stored in an airtight tin for about four to five weeks and used as and when needed. For this recipe you need a deep frying pan or wok.

Cooking and preparation time: 12 hours *Makes:* about 1.35kg (3 lb)

450g (1 lb) dried split chick peas
1200ml (2 pt) cooking oil for frying
225g (8 oz) puffed rice
225g (8 oz) ready salted crisps
225g (8 oz) ready salted peanuts
1 tsp salt
1 tsp turmeric powder
1 tsp chilli powder

1. Soak the split peas in about 2 litres (3½ pt) of water overnight.
2. Drain off all the water from the split peas and spread on kitchen roll paper.
3. Heat the oil in a large wok or frying pan to a high temperature. Place small amounts of the split peas in the oil, and deep fry until they are golden brown, or are hard and crunchy when tasted. Remove the split peas with a sieve and spread the fried peas on some fresh kitchen roll paper. Fry all the split peas in this way.

4. Now fry the rice in the hot oil, again only a small quantity at a time. Puffed rice grains fry very quickly, so keep the pot and sieve ready.

5. Mix the fried rice, split peas, crisps, peanuts, salt, turmeric powder and chilli powder in a large pot. Mix well, and transfer the contents to an airtight tin. This will keep the Chavada fresh for about a month.

6. Serve as and when needed, making sure that the lid of the tin is kept well closed, after use.

SAVOURY PEANUTS

Indians like spices in most of their snacks, and peanuts are no exception. They are usually served at parties, or with a glass of wine or a cup of tea. Savoury peanuts can be stored in an airtight tin for up to three weeks, and used as and when needed. For this recipe you need a wok or deep frying pan.

Cooking and preparation time: 20 minutes

Makes: about 900g (2 lb) peanuts

600ml (1 pt) cooking oil
900g (2 lb) unsalted peanuts
1 tsp salt
1 tsp chilli powder
1 tsp black pepper powder

1. Heat the oil to a high temperature, in a wok or deep frying pan. Once the oil is hot, reduce the heat and add a handful of peanuts. Deep fry until they are golden brown. This will usually take about 10 to 15 seconds. Remove the peanuts with a sieve and spread them on kitchen roll paper.

2. Repeat this with all the peanuts.

3. In a large mixing bowl, mix well the peanuts, salt, chilli powder and pepper powder.

4. Let the peanuts cool, and then transfer the contents to an airtight tin. They can be stored this way for up to three weeks.

SAVOURY CASHEW NUTS

Savoury cashew nuts taste excellent and are well worth a try. Like peanuts, they are usually served at parties, or with a glass of wine or a cup of tea. They can be stored in an airtight tin for up to two weeks, and used as and when needed. For this recipe you need a wok or deep frying pan.

Cooking and preparation time: 20 minutes

Makes: about 900g (2 lb) cashew nuts

600ml (1 pt) cooking oil
900g (2 lb) cashew nuts
1 tsp salt
1 tsp chilli powder
1 tsp black pepper powder

1. Heat the oil to a high temperature, in a wok or a deep frying pan. Once the oil is hot, reduce the heat and add a handful of cashew nuts. Deep fry until they are golden brown. This will usually take about 10 to 15 seconds. Remove the cashew nuts with a sieve and spread them on kitchen roll paper.
2. Repeat this with all the cashew nuts.
3. In a large mixing bowl, mix the cashew nuts, salt, chilli powder and pepper powder well together.
4. Let the cashew nuts cool, and then transfer the contents to an airtight tin. They can be stored this way for up to two weeks.

KHARI PURIS

A savoury snack that will keep for weeks in an airtight container. It can be served as a snack on its own or with drinks.

Cooking and preparation time: 50 minutes   *Serves:* several

450g (1 lb) plain flour
125ml (¼ pt) warm oil
115g (4 oz) gram flour
1 tbsp cumin seeds
1 tsp salt
1 tsp black pepper, coarsely ground
cold water for binding
oil for deep frying

1. Mix all the ingredients together (*except* for the frying oil) and bind using just enough water to create a firm dough.
2. Heat the oil for deep frying.
3. Roll out the dough into a very thin, large circle.
4. Cut into triangles, prick with a fork and deep fry until golden brown.
5. Drain on kitchen roll paper.

POTATO POUWA

This is a snack made from spiced potato and flaked rice. It can be served almost any time of day. Some people have it for breakfast, some have it at tea time and some even have it as a light lunch or supper. It is an ideal dish to make when unexpected guests arrive.

Cooking and preparation time: 20–30 minutes   *Serves:* 4

450g (1 lb) potatoes, cubed
6 tbsp cooking oil
1 tsp mustard seeds
1 tsp cumin seeds
2 tsp salt
2 tsp ground turmeric
115g (4 oz) flaked rice
5 green chillies
3 cloves garlic
1 tbsp sesame seeds
juice of 1 lemon
2 tbsp green coriander, chopped

1. Peel the potatoes and cut into 2.5cm (1 in) cubes. Heat the oil in a large frying pan. When hot, add the mustard seeds and cumin seeds, cover and allow to 'pop' for a few seconds. Then add the potato cubes to the pan taking great care as this will make the oil splatter.
2. Add the salt and turmeric, stir, cover and reduce the heat to medium. Cook, covered, until the potato cubes are just tender. Stir several times during cooking.
3. In the meantime, rinse the flaked rice with warm water and drain. Mince the green chillies and garlic and add to the potato in the pan. Sprinkle the sesame seeds and stir well. (If you've handled the chillies, make sure you wash your hands well.)
4. Cook with the lid off for 1 minute, then add the drained flaked rice and mix well.
5. Cover and cook for 2 minutes over very gentle heat. Add the lemon juice and chopped coriander and mix everything once again. Adjust the salt if necessary.

HANDVA

This is a savoury, spicy 'cake' type snack made from rice flour, usually served at high teas, parties or picnics. It can be stored in the fridge for a couple of days and heated as and when required. For this recipe you need a liquidiser, a whisk and a 20cm (8 in) cake tin.

Cooking and preparation time: 50 hours   *Serves:* 4

90ml (3 fl oz) natural yoghurt
90ml (3 fl oz) water
340g (12 oz) dhokra flour (see Glossary)
25g (1 oz) fresh garlic, peeled
3 green chillies
1 tsp salt
1 tsp turmeric powder
½ tsp chilli powder
¼ tsp baking powder
60ml (2 fl oz) cooking oil
¼ tsp cumin seeds
¼ tsp black mustard seeds
¼ tsp asafoetida

1. Mix the yoghurt and water together with a whisk. This mixture is called 'lassi'.
2. Mix the dhokra flour and lassi together well, and leave to ferment in a warm spot, for 48 hours. The airing cupboard is ideal for this purpose.
3. Place the garlic and chillies into a liquidiser, and chop very finely.
4. After fermentation, add the salt, turmeric powder, chilli powder, baking powder and liquidiser contents to the dhokra mixture. Mix well.
5. Heat the oil in a frying pan to a high temperature, and add the cumin and black mustard seeds and asafoetida. Cook for a few seconds.
6. Transfer half of the heated oil mixture to a 20cm (8 in) cake tin. Add the dhokra flour mixture and then pour the remaining oil mixture on top of the dhokra mixture.

(continued overleaf)

7. Bake in a preheated oven at 150°C (300°F), gas mark 2, for about 2½ hours on the middle shelf of the oven.

8. Leave the Handva to cool for a few minutes and then cut into small pieces for serving. The cut pieces can be stored in a fridge, and warmed when needed (for about 20 minutes, in a preheated oven) before serving.

AFRICAN RICE CAKES

Absolutely delicious – just try them! It is best to eat them within a few days, as a snack.

Cooking and preparation time: 3–4 hours   *Serves:* 6
                                        plus overnight soaking

450g (1 lb) fat grain rice (pudding rice)
55g (2 oz) coconut cream
250ml (½ pt) boiling water
500ml (1 pt) milk
225g (8 oz) sugar
2 tsp cardamom seeds, coarsely ground
4 tsp dried yeast
1 egg
oil for frying

1. Soak the rice for 2–3 hours.
2. Melt the coconut cream in boiling water.
3. Drain the rice and mix with the coconut cream, milk, sugar, cardamom seeds and yeast, cover and leave overnight.
4. The next day, add the egg and mix together.
5. Heat some oil in a frying pan and shallow fry one tablespoon of the mixture at a time, turning, until both sides are brown.

NOORI BISCUITS

A type of shortbread-like biscuit to snack as you please, or serve as an accompaniment with ice-cream.

Cooking and preparation time: 50 minutes   *Serves:* several

150g (5 oz) butter
115g (4 oz) sugar
1 egg
150g (5 oz) plain flour
½ tsp baking powder
1 tsp ground nutmeg
115g (4 oz) ground almonds
115g (4 oz) fine semolina
whole almonds to decorate

1. Cream the butter and sugar until pale.
2. Add the egg and whisk gently.
3. Sieve the flour, baking powder, ground nutmeg, ground almonds and semolina into the mixture and fold gently into a soft dough.
4. Take small balls the size of walnuts and flatten, then decorate with three almonds before placing on a greased baking tray.
5. Cook in a pre-heated oven at 180°C (350°F), gas mark 4, for 20 minutes, until just golden brown.

MANDAZI

An African-style bread snack, deep fried until golden brown and sprinkled with desiccated coconut. Best eaten hot or will keep for weeks in an airtight container. Serve hot for breakfast or cold as a snack at tea time or in between meals.

Cooking and preparation time: 1 hour 40 minutes   *Serves:* 6

450g (1 lb) plain flour
6 tbsp sugar (or to taste)
55g (2 oz) coconut cream, dissolved in a little boiling water
4 tsp cardamom seeds, coarsely ground
1 tsp butter
1 tbsp dried yeast
1 tsp baking powder
oil for deep frying
desiccated coconut

1. Mix all the ingredients (*except* the oil and desiccated coconut) into a dough.
2. Cover and leave in a warm place to rise and double in size either overnight or for at least 40 minutes.
3. Knead the dough and roll out to 1cm (⅓ in) thick.
4. Heat the oil.
5. Cut the dough into diamonds or shapes of your choice and fry until golden brown.
6. Drain on kitchen roll paper.
7. Sprinkle with desiccated coconut while hot.

THEPLAS

These are a type of doughnut that can be stored for several weeks and eaten as a snack at your leisure! They go well with a cup of tea.

Cooking and preparation time: 1 hour   *Serves:* several

450g (1 lb) plain flour
115g (4 oz) brown sugar
3 tsp cardamom seeds, coarsely ground
2 tbsp oil
1 tsp baking powder
handful fennel seeds
hot water, as required
oil for frying

1. Mix all the ingredients (*except* the oil for frying) with just enough hot water to bind into a dough.
2. Heat the oil.
3. In the meantime, roll out the dough into a large circle, 0.5cm (¼ in) thick, and cut into any shapes that you desire.
4. Deep fry until golden brown and drain on kitchen roll paper.

Note: cool before storing.

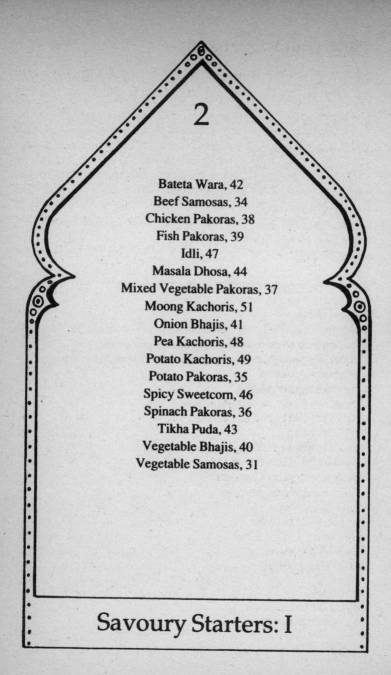

2

Bateta Wara, 42
Beef Samosas, 34
Chicken Pakoras, 38
Fish Pakoras, 39
Idli, 47
Masala Dhosa, 44
Mixed Vegetable Pakoras, 37
Moong Kachoris, 51
Onion Bhajis, 41
Pea Kachoris, 48
Potato Kachoris, 49
Potato Pakoras, 35
Spicy Sweetcorn, 46
Spinach Pakoras, 36
Tikha Puda, 43
Vegetable Bhajis, 40
Vegetable Samosas, 31

Savoury Starters: I

VEGETABLE SAMOSAS

Triangular pastries with vegetable fillings and deep fried until golden brown, Samosas can be served hot or cold as a starter with salad, a wedge of lemon and a dip of chutney, or with Green Coriander and Coconut Chutney to pour over (see page 234).

The stuffing is quite simple to make, but if you are new to Indian cookery you may find the thin pastry difficult. You can always cheat by using Chinese spring roll pastry. You will find this in Chinese food shops. It comes in a stack of frozen squares. To use, defrost at room temperature and gently separate the thin sheets of pastry and cut each in half, forming even rectangles. Chinese pastry will do the job but it is never as good as proper samosa pastry. Be brave and try making some.

For this recipe you need a flat frying pan or tavi and a deep frying pan or wok.

Cooking and preparation time: 1 hour   *Serves:* 6

For the filling
2 tbsp oil
2 medium sized onions, finely chopped
  ***or* 2 bunches of spring onions, finely chopped**
4 tsp garlic, crushed
4 tsp ginger, grated
115g (4 oz) finely cubed potatoes
115g (4 oz) finely cubed carrots
55g (2 oz) peas
3 or more green chillies, finely chopped
handful of fresh coriander, chopped
2 tsp garam masala powder
1 tsp turmeric powder
juice of 1 lemon
chilli powder to taste
salt to taste
60ml (2 fl oz) water
oil for deep frying

For the paste
2 tbsp plain flour
water for binding

(continued overleaf)

For the pastry
450g (1 lb) plain flour
1 tsp salt
1 tsp oil
1 tsp lemon juice
cold water
plain flour, in a dredger
10–12 tbsp oil for brushing
oil for deep frying

1. Heat the oil and add the onions.
2. When the onions have softened, add the garlic and ginger and fry for 5 minutes.
3. Then add all the other ingredients (except for the oil for deep frying), cover and simmer for 40 minutes until all the vegetables have gone mushy. Allow to cool.
4. Meanwhile, make the pastry by first sifting the flour and salt into a bowl. Rub in the oil and lemon juice and add enough cold water to bind into a soft pliable dough. Divide the dough into walnut-sized pieces. Flatten each piece between the palms of your hands and roll out on a floured board to approximately 7–8cm (3 in) in diameter.
5. Do this with the rest of the dough, spreading them all out on a clean tray or work surface. Brush oil liberally over all the dough discs and sprinkle with the flour from the flour dredger. Pair up the discs with the oiled and floured sides facing.
6. Now set your tavi or non-stick frying pan over a low heat. Roll out each pair of discs carefully on a floured board taking care not to allow the dough to pleat as you roll. Roll as thin as you can, keeping the round shape.
7. Cook on the heated tavi or frying pan, turning quickly as soon as little bubbles are seen to appear. Separate out the two layers carefully and stack with the spotted sides down. This operation takes literally seconds. It is very important not to over cook the pastry at this stage as it will be cooked again later. Wrap them in a clean tea towel as you cook others to keep them soft.
8. When all the pastry is cooked in this way re-stack them on a chopping board, making a neat pile. Now trim off the two opposite edges of the pastry stack, as shown in the diagram, leaving something resembling a square. Make another cut in the centre making

two stacks of long strips. The trimmed off edges can be fried and served with drinks.

9. Adjust the seasoning in the now cold filling and fill the samosas as follows. First make a paste of flour and water to stick the pastry envelopes down (1 tablespoon plain flour and 1 tablespoon water). Taking a strip of pastry with the long edge to your right, fold along line AB. Brush the paste along the edge B to C and bring A to meet C. Press down to stick. Fill the resulting envelope with some of the filling and wrap the flap over and secure with more paste.

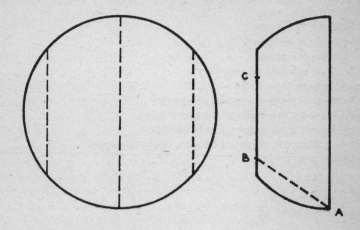

Make all the samosas in this way and spread out on a tray until ready to fry. Deep fry at medium heat until crisp and golden. Drain on absorbent kitchen roll paper.

Note: if there are any holes the samosa will become oil-logged and lose its filling as well as its taste during frying.

(If you are new to folding samosas it may help you to fold a strip of paper as per the directions before trying with the pastry strips.)

BEEF SAMOSAS

These Indian beef pastries can be served as a savoury snack at parties or with high teas, or as a starter with salad, a wedge of lemon and a dip or chutney. Like vegetable samosas they are useful for picnics. Raw filled samosas can be stored in a freezer and then fried when needed. For this recipe you need a flat frying pan or tavi and a deep frying pan or wok.

Cooking and preparation time: 1 hour   *Serves:* 6

For the filling
300g (11 oz) mince
4 tsp garlic, crushed
4 tsp ginger, grated
2 tsp garam masala powder
salt to taste
handful of fresh coriander, chopped
3 or more green chillies, finely chopped
2 medium sized onions, finely chopped
  ***or* 2 bunches of spring onions, finely chopped**
oil for deep frying

For the paste
2 tbsp plain flour
water for binding

For the pastry
450g (1 lb) plain flour
1 tsp salt
1 tsp oil
1 tsp lemon juice
cold water
plain flour, in a dredger
10–12 tbsp oil for brushing
oil for deep frying

1. Dry cook the mince (without any oil) in a non-stick pan.
2. Add the garlic, ginger, garam masala and salt and stir.
3. Remove from the heat, allow to cool, add the coriander, chillies and onions.
4. Meanwhile, make the pastry and fill the samosas by following steps 4–9 of Vegetable Samosas (page 32).

Note: wash hands thoroughly after handling chillies.

POTATO PAKORAS

Thinly sliced potatoes in gram flour batter make another savoury snack which can be served at high teas. It is also a good starter to a main meal. Potato lovers will enjoy this dish. Most children are very fond of potato pakoras. For this recipe you need a deep frying pan or wok.

Cooking and preparation time: 30 minutes   *Serves:* 4

170g (6 oz) gram flour
120ml (4 fl oz) water
340g (12 oz) potatoes, peeled and sliced finely, similar to crisps,
    but slightly thicker
¾ tsp garlic powder
¾ tsp salt
¾ tsp chilli powder
¾ tsp garam masala
¾ tsp turmeric powder
600ml (1 pt) cooking oil for frying

1. Sieve the gram flour into a mixing bowl.
2. Mix the flour, water, potatoes, garlic powder, salt, chilli powder, garam masala, and turmeric powder well.
3. Heat the cooking oil to a high temperature in a wok or deep frying pan. Pick each potato piece individually from the mixture and place it in the hot oil until you have about ten pieces. The pakoras will float in the oil, and each side should be deep fried until it is golden orange. With a sieve, drain the pakoras and place them on absorbent kitchen roll paper.
4. Repeat with the remaining pakoras and serve while hot.

SPINACH PAKORAS

Sliced spinach in gram flour batter can be served at high teas. It is also a good starter to a main meal. Spinach lovers will really enjoy spinach pakoras. For this recipe you will need a deep frying pan or wok.

Cooking and preparation time: 30 minutes　　　　　　　*Serves:* 4

115g (4 oz) gram flour
55g (2 oz) spinach, finely chopped
90ml (3 fl oz) water
¾ tsp salt
¾ tsp chilli powder
3 green chillies, finely chopped
¾ tsp turmeric powder
600ml (1 pt) cooking oil for frying

1. Sieve the gram flour into a mixing bowl.
2. Mix the flour, spinach, water, salt, chilli powder, chillies and turmeric powder well.
3. Heat the cooking oil to a high temperature in a wok or deep frying pan. Take a teaspoonful of the spinach mixture and place it gently in the hot oil. Repeat this until you have about ten pieces in the oil. After a few seconds the pieces will float to the top of the oil. Then fry each side of the spinach pakora until it is golden orange. This frying process should take about 4–5 minutes; any quicker and the oil is too hot and therefore the heat should be lowered. With a sieve, drain the pakoras and place them on kitchen roll paper.
4. Repeat with the remaining spinach mixture.
5. Transfer the pakoras to a serving dish and serve while hot.

MIXED VEGETABLE PAKORAS

Onions, potatoes and spinach in gram flour batter is a savoury dish which can be used as a starter or a snack and can be served with high teas or at parties. For this recipe you will need a liquidiser or blender and a deep frying pan or wok.

Cooking and preparation time: 40 minutes   *Serves:* 4

10g (½ oz) fresh garlic, peeled
10g (½ oz) fresh ginger, peeled
5 green chillies
170g (6 oz) gram flour
2 potatoes, peeled and finely chopped
85g (3 oz) fresh spinach, finely chopped
1 large onion, finely chopped
1 tsp chilli powder
1 tsp tandoori masala
1 tsp garam masala
1 tsp salt
1 tsp turmeric powder
120ml (4 fl oz) water
600ml (1 pt) cooking oil for frying

1. Put the garlic, ginger and green chillies into a liquidiser and chop finely.
2. Sieve the gram flour into a mixing bowl and mix in the contents of the liquidiser, potatoes, spinach, onion, chilli powder, tandoori masala, garam masala, salt, turmeric powder and water. Mix everything well.
3. Heat the oil to a high temperature in a wok or deep frying pan. Add about 10 tablespoonfuls of the mixture, a tablespoonful at a time, to the heated oil. These will float and should be deep fried for about 3–4 minutes, until each of the fried pakoras is golden brown.
4. Remove the pakoras with a sieve and drain the excess oil off them by placing the pakoras on kitchen roll paper.
5. Repeat with the remaining pakoras and serve while hot.

CHICKEN PAKORAS

Chicken pieces in gram flour batter can be served at high teas, parties or even picnics. For this recipe you need a deep frying pan or wok.

Cooking and preparation time: 1 hour   *Serves:* 4

450g (1 lb) frozen chicken pieces (thawed)
115g (4 oz) gram flour
120ml (4 fl oz) water
½ tsp salt
½ tsp chilli powder
½ tsp garam masala
½ tsp turmeric powder
2 tsp soy sauce
600ml (1 pt) cooking oil for frying

1. Remove the skin of the chicken pieces and cut the flesh from the bones. Cut the flesh into about 2cm (1 in) cubes.
2. Bake these chicken cubes in a preheated oven at 180°C (350°F), gas mark 4, for about 20 minutes. Remove the pieces from the oven and allow them to cool.
3. Sieve the gram flour into a mixing bowl.
4. Mix the flour, water, salt, chilli powder, garam masala, turmeric powder, and soy sauce well to form a thickish paste.
5. Heat the cooking oil to a high temperature in a wok or deep frying pan. Dip each chicken piece individually in the paste and place it in the hot oil until you have about five pieces. After a few seconds the chicken pakoras will float to the top of the oil. Deep fry each side of the pakora until it is golden orange. This will usually take about 2 minutes for each side. With a sieve, drain the pakoras and place them on kitchen roll paper.
6. Repeat with the remaining chicken pieces and serve while hot.

FISH PAKORAS

This savoury snack of fish pieces in gram flour batter, which can be served at high teas, parties or even picnics, could also be served with chips, instead of the traditional English fish and chips. For this recipe you need a deep frying pan or wok.

Cooking and preparation time: 1 hour   *Serves:* 4

450g (1 lb) cod fillets
115g (4 oz) gram flour
120ml (4 fl oz) water
½ tsp salt
½ tsp chilli powder
½ tsp garam masala
½ tsp turmeric powder
2 tsp soy sauce
600ml (1 pt) cooking oil for frying

1. Cut the fillets into pieces about 5cm (2 in) long and about 1cm (½ in) wide.
2. Sieve the gram flour into a mixing bowl.
3. Mix the flour, water, salt, chilli powder, garam masala, turmeric powder, and soy sauce well to form a thickish paste.
4. Heat the cooking oil to a high temperature in a wok or deep frying pan. Lower the heat and leave it for a further 3–4 minutes. Dip each fish piece individually in the paste and place it in the hot oil until you have about 5 pieces. After a few seconds the fish pakoras will float to the top of the oil. Deep fry each side of the pakora until it is golden orange. This will usually take about 4 minutes for each side. With a sieve, drain the fish pakoras and place them on kitchen roll paper.
5. Repeat with the remaining fish pieces and serve while hot.

VEGETABLE BHAJIS

These are fritters made with any vegetable of your choice, such as sliced potatoes, aubergines or mushrooms; cauliflower heads; sliced capsicum peppers; or green chillies split lengthways. Serve as a starter with a dip or chutney, or as spicy snacks to be served with drinks. They are best eaten straightaway but they can be prepared ahead and served cold if wished. They're also good with ready-made mango chutney. Try this recipe with thickly sliced bananas instead of one of the suggested vegetables for a delicious alternative.

Cooking and preparation time: 40 minutes   *Serves:* 4

150g (5 oz) gram flour
1 tsp celery seeds
1 tsp cumin seeds
4 tsp garlic, crushed
2 tsp ginger, grated
¼ tsp baking powder
1 medium sized onion, sliced
handful of fresh coriander and fenugreek leaves, chopped
1 small potato, finely sliced or coarsely grated
handful of other vegetables of your choice
1 tsp salt (or to taste)
water
oil for deep frying

1. Mix all the ingredients (*except* the oil) with small amounts of water until a batter of dropping consistency is formed.
2. Heat the oil for frying and add a tablespoon of this hot oil to the batter mixture.
3. Take a tablespoon of the batter and fry until golden brown.
4. Drain on kitchen roll paper.

Note: wash hands thoroughly after handling chillies.

ONION BHAJIS

Onion rings fried in gram flour batter make one of the many Indian starter dishes. They can also be used as a snack served with a glass of wine or other drinks. For this recipe you will need a liquidiser and a deep frying pan or wok.

Cooking and preparation time: 40 minutes   *Serves:* 4

10g (½ oz) fresh ginger, peeled
10g (½ oz) fresh garlic, peeled
4 green chillies
85g (3 oz) gram flour
½ tsp salt
½ tsp chilli powder
½ tsp garam masala
½ tsp tandoori masala
90ml (3 fl oz) water
2 largish onions, cut into rings
600ml (1 pt) cooking oil for deep frying

1. Put the ginger, garlic and green chillies into a liquidiser and process until very finely chopped.
2. Sieve the gram flour into a mixing bowl. Add the contents of the liquidiser, salt, chilli powder, garam masala, tandoori masala and mix well. Add the water and mix well again into a thickish, smooth batter.
3. Add the onion rings to the batter and mix gently so that the onions are well covered with batter.
4. Heat the oil to a high temperature in a small wok, or deep frying pan. When the oil is hot, remove the onion rings one at a time from the batter and deep fry in the oil. This method of frying onions is similar to frying chips or fish in batter. Fry only six to seven rings at a time.
5. Serve the onion bhajis while they are still hot.

BATETA WARA

These are a type of potato fritter. Serve hot with some tamarind or tomato ketchup.

Cooking and preparation time: 1 hour   *Serves:* 6

450g (1 lb) potatoes, boiled and mashed
4 tsp garlic, crushed
4 tsp ginger, grated
1 tsp turmeric powder
1 tsp chilli powder
handful of coriander leaves, chopped
juice of 1 lemon
salt to taste
oil for deep frying

For batter
115g (4 oz) gram flour
125ml (¼ pt) water
pinch of salt
½ tsp chilli powder

1. To make the potato balls, mix all the ingredients (*except* the oil) with the mashed potatoes, and roll into equal sized balls (actual size depending on your preference).
2. Mix all the batter ingredients together.
3. Heat the oil for frying.
4. Dip the balls into the batter then deep fry until golden brown and drain on kitchen roll paper.

TIKHA PUDA

These spicy pancakes are usually served as a snack with a cup of tea. Eat them as they are or spread a tablespoon of honey over them for a sweet and spicy taste. You could also serve them for the first course at a dinner party, in which case serve with Spicy Yoghurt Chutney (see page 238) to pour over the Puda. Left-over Puda mixture can be refrigerated. Use within two days.

Preparation time: 10 minutes plus 6 hours proving time
Cooking time: 2 minutes each   *Serves:* 8–10

450g (1 lb) gram flour
225g (8 oz) coarse cornflour
55g (2 oz) wholewheat flour
2.5cm (1 in) root ginger
4 green chillies
3 cloves garlic
2 tsp salt
1 tsp ground turmeric
1 tbsp ground coriander
1 tsp granulated sugar
5 tbsp natural yoghurt
6 tbsp cooking oil
warm water
either: 1 bunch fresh fenugreek, chopped
or: 1 green pawpaw, grated
or: 1 large onion, finely chopped
oil for cooking

1. In a large bowl, combine all the ingredients (except your chosen vegetable) and enough warm water to make a batter consistency. Leave in a warm place for at least 6 hours. Remember to wash your hands after handling the chillies.
2. When you are ready to make the Puda, mix into your batter one of the vegetables suggested.
3. Heat a tavi or a frying pan on medium heat. Brush about a teaspoon of oil over it and pour a ladleful of batter into the tavi. Spread the batter with the back of a spoon into a round shape. Cover and leave for 1 minute. Using a flat object like a spatula,

(continued overleaf)

gently ease the Puda off the tavi and flip over to cook the other side. Pour a teaspoon of oil along the edge of the Puda so that the oil can go under the Puda to cook and brown the other side (about 1 minute).

4. When both sides are done, remove the Puda from the tavi and keep warm.

5. Make as many as required. Any left-over batter can be kept in the refrigerator for a couple of days.

MASALA DHOSA

These stuffed pancakes make a good dish for a dinner party and it is easy to double the quantities given here if you wish to serve a larger number of people. Alternatively, you might like to double the quantity and freeze the left-over batter, after proving for 24 hours, so that you have some in store. Do make sure you use a large bowl to mix the batter ingredients and leave it in a warm place, but not too hot, as it may froth and spill over if the bowl is too small or the temperature is too high. To use the frozen batter, just defrost at room temperature for 4–5 hours and then follow the recipe for making the pancakes. It is not advisable to freeze the filling, so make fresh filling when it is needed.

To make a delicious supper or a first course at a dinner party, serve these covered with Sambhar and a tablespoon of Spicy Yoghurt Chutney (see pages 202 and 238).

Cooking and preparation time: 24 hours + 15–20 minutes

Serves: 6–8

Dhosa Batter
450g (1 lb) rice flour
115g (4 oz) urid flour
½ tsp salt
1 tbsp natural yoghurt
warm water

Filling
1 large potato
1 large onion
2 tbsp oil
½ tsp mustard seeds
½ tsp cumin seeds
1 tsp salt
½ tsp ground turmeric
½ tsp chilli powder
1 tbsp ground coriander
½ tsp granulated sugar

oil for making dhosas

1. Mix the batter ingredients together using enough warm water to make a porridge-like consistency, cover and leave in a warm place for 24 hours.
2. To make the filling: peel and chop both the potato and onion coarsely, but keep them separate. Heat the oil in a frying pan, add the mustard and cumin seeds and cover the pan. When they have stopped 'popping', add the potato, salt and turmeric. Mix well, reduce the heat and cook, covered, for 5 minutes. Add the onion, chilli powder, ground coriander and sugar, mix thoroughly and cook with the lid on for a further 10 minutes, stirring occasionally.
3. To make the dhosa: heat 1 tablespoon of oil in a frying pan (preferably non-stick) over a medium to high heat. Pour a ladleful of the batter into the middle and tip the frying pan from side to side in order to spread the batter. Cook for 1 minute and then turn over using a spatula and cook the other side for 30 seconds. Turn out onto a serving plate, put some filling in the middle and fold like a pancake.

SPICY SWEETCORN

This is a favourite snack dish because it is quick, easy and delicious. Serve it with some home-made natural yoghurt and Sev (see page 16). Sev can also be bought ready-made from many Indian grocery shops. This dish can be served very successfully as a first course at a dinner party.

Cooking and preparation time: 7–12 minutes   *Serves:* 6

2 × 510g (1 lb 2 oz) cans sweetcorn
6 tbsp cooking oil
2 tsp mustard seeds
2 tsp cumin seeds
1 tsp ground turmeric
3 cloves garlic
3–4 green chillies
6 heaped tbsp natural yoghurt
3 tbsp green coriander, chopped
Sev to serve (see page 16)

1. Open the cans of sweetcorn. Heat the oil in a heavy based pan. Add the mustard and cumin seeds and cover the pan. Allow to 'pop' for a few seconds then add the contents of the cans, holding the lid ready to cover quickly. Be careful when you do this as the hot oil may splatter.
2. Uncover the pan after a minute, reduce the heat to medium, add the turmeric and mix well.
3. Cook, uncovered, for about 5 minutes or until nearly all the liquid has evaporated.
4. In the meantime, mince the chillies and garlic together. Add to the pan and cook for a further minute. (Remember to wash your hands thoroughly after handling the chillies.) Stir in the yoghurt and chopped coriander.
5. Adjust the seasoning and serve in bowls sprinkled with a handful of Sev.

IDLI

Idli originates from the south of India where people are poor and cannot afford to eat the highly priced rice grain, so instead they use rice flour made from inferior quality rice and make steamed rice cakes from it. These are worth trying.

For this recipe you will need a double steamer and an Idli stand. An Idli stand is a three-tiered utensil with four hollows in each tier, a little like a bun tin. The Idli batter is poured into each hollow (as you would with Yorkshire Pudding batter) and then the whole stand is put inside the double steamer to cook the Idli.

If you wish to buy an Idli stand there are some shops that specialise in utensils used for Indian cookery, but, of course, it is always possible to improvise. If you have a shallow metal tray or dish that will fit comfortably in the steamer, then you can use it to cook your Idli in. When cooked, cut into diamond shapes and ease out of the tray or dish with a flat implement. Serve in deep plates or bowls with a ladleful of Sambhar poured over (see page 202). Lastly, spoon some Spicy Yoghurt Chutney (page 238) over the Sambhar for a final touch.

This is a wonderful dinner party starter dish with a difference.

Cooking and preparation time: 24 hours + 30 minutes   *Serves:* 8

775g (1 lb 11 oz) rice flour
225g (8 oz) urid flour
1½ tsp salt
4 tbsp oil
warm water
Eno's fruit salt (available from most chemists)

1. Put the two different flours with the salt and oil in a glass bowl. Add enough warm water to make a thick porridge-like consistency. Cover and leave in a warm place for 24 hours.
2. Put some water in the bottom of a double steamer and bring to the boil. If you do not have an Idli stand, a metal tin that fits into the steamer will do. Oil well.
3. Take two ladlefuls of the batter in a bowl and add 1 teaspoon of Eno's fruit salt. Quickly mix and fill the Idli tins or whatever is being used. The batter will spread and take the shape of the container. Steam for 10 minutes. Remove and keep warm. Use up all the batter using 1 teaspoon of Eno's fruit salt with each batch.
4. If Idli is cooked in a tin, cut into diamond shapes before serving.

PEA KACHORIS

These stuffed patties are little round dough parcels with a spicy savoury filling. They may be served with drinks or with a cup of Gujarati-style tea (see page 276) and some fried poppadums. They also make a wonderful first course. Simply lay two or three Kachoris on a bed of shredded lettuce and pour over a little Green Coriander and Coconut Chutney (page 234). It is best to use fresh peas in this recipe.

Cooking and preparation time: 7–20 minutes   *Serves:* 4–6

Filling
225g (8 oz) shelled peas
8 tbsp cooking oil
1 tsp mustard seeds
1 tsp cumin seeds
¼ tsp asafoetida powder
1–1½ tsp salt
1 tsp ground turmeric
3–4 green chillies
2 cloves garlic
2 tbsp desiccated coconut
1 tbsp sesame seeds
juice of 1 lemon

Dough
125g (4 oz) plain flour
½ tsp salt
1 tbsp cooking oil
tepid water

extra oil for frying

1. To make the filling: wash and mince the peas. Heat the oil in a large non-stick frying pan. Add the mustard and cumin seeds and allow to 'pop' with the lid on. Add the asafoetida powder, the minced peas, salt and turmeric. Mix well and cook for 5-7 minutes with the lid off.
2. Mince the chillies and the garlic together and add to the pan. Stir fry for 1 minute. Now add the desiccated coconut and the sesame seeds and continue to stir fry for another minute. (Wash your hands thoroughly after handling the chillies!)

3. Lastly, add the lemon juice and mix thoroughly. Adjust the seasoning if required. Remove from the heat and allow to cool completely.

4. To make the dough: sift the flour and salt into a bowl. Add the oil and rub in. Now add enough tepid water to form a soft dough.

5. Divide the dough into walnut-sized balls. Roll a ball of dough out to a 8cm (3 in) circle. Place a tablespoon of the filling in the centre and very carefully bring up the sides and press together at the top, enclosing the filling. Slightly flatten the shape and put aside. Repeat the process with the rest of the dough.

6. Now set the oil to heat over a low to medium heat. Do not allow the oil to get too hot. Lower a few kachoris into the oil and cook, turning occasionally until lightly browned all over. Drain on absorbent kitchen roll paper. Repeat until all the kachoris have been fried. Serve hot or cold.

POTATO KACHORIS

This is a dish of potato balls that is very similar to samosas, but the pastry is made of chapatti flour, rather than plain flour. It can be served as a starter or at high teas and parties. Any left-over filling can be used for toasted sandwiches. For this recipe you need a deep frying pan or wok.

Cooking and preparation time: 1 hour   *Makes:* about 8 kachoris

For filling
30ml (1 fl oz) cooking oil
½ tsp black mustard seeds
1 large onion, finely chopped
450g (1 lb) peeled potatoes, finely diced
1 tsp salt
1 tsp turmeric powder
1 tsp chilli powder
60ml (2 fl oz) water
15ml (½ fl oz) lemon juice

(continued overleaf)

For pastry
225g (8 oz) white chapatti flour, sieved
120ml (4 fl oz) water
55g (2 oz) chapatti flour for rolling out
600ml (1 pt) cooking oil for frying

1. In a pan, heat the oil to a high temperature. Add the black mustard seeds and let them cook for a few seconds. Add the onion and cook until the onion is golden brown. Add the potatoes, salt, turmeric powder and chilli powder. Stir and cook for about 2 minutes.
2. Add the 60ml (2 fl oz) of water, lower the heat, cover the pan and allow it to simmer for about 10 minutes. Then add the lemon juice, mix well, and switch off the heat. Let it cool.
3. Place the chapatti flour in a big bowl; add half of the 120ml (4 fl oz) of water and mix well. Continue adding small amounts of water at a time and mixing well until a soft, medium dough is formed. Divide this dough into roughly eight equal pieces. Shape these pieces into round balls.
4. Sprinkle some dry flour onto each ball, and roll it into a circle about 13cm (5 in) in diameter. Place 4 teaspoonsfuls of the potato filling in the middle of one half of the rolled chapatti. Lift the other half to cover the filling completely and squeeze the edges together thus making a semi-circle shape with the filling in the middle. Lift it carefully and place it on one side. Repeat this with all the eight balls. These filled balls are called kachoris.
5. Heat the 600ml (1 pt) of oil to a high temperature, in a deep frying pan or wok. Now add two kachoris at a time and fry each side of the kachori until it is golden brown. This will usually take about 3–4 minutes for each side. Fry all the kachoris in this way.
6. Serve the kachoris while they are hot.

MOONG KACHORIS

The pastry for these mung bean balls is made of chapatti flour, rather than plain flour. Moong Kachoris are popular with vegetarians and can be served as a starter or at high teas and parties. Any leftover filling can be used for toasted sandwiches. For this recipe you need a deep frying pan or wok.

Cooking and preparation time: 10 hours   *Makes:* about 8 kachoris

For filling
225g (8 oz) skinless, split mung beans
1200ml (2 pt) water for soaking
30ml (1 fl oz) cooking oil
½ tsp black mustard seeds
½ tsp cumin seeds
1½ tsp salt
1 tsp turmeric powder
1 tsp chilli powder
1 tsp garam masala
300ml (½ pt) water
30ml (1 fl oz) lemon juice

For pastry
225g (8 oz) white chapatti flour, sieved
120ml (4 fl oz) water
55g (2 oz) chapatti flour for rolling out
600ml (1 pt) cooking oil for frying

1. Wash the split beans making sure that little stones are not left in.
2. Soak the beans overnight in the water.
3. Drain the water from the beans in the morning.
4. In a pan, heat the oil to a high temperature. Add the black mustard seeds and cumin seeds and cook for a few seconds. Add the beans, salt, turmeric powder, chilli powder and garam masala. Stir and cook for about 2 minutes.
5. Add the 300ml (½ pt) of water, lower the heat, cover the pan and allow it to simmer for about 20 minutes. Now add the lemon juice, mix well and switch off the heat. Let this filling cool down.
6. Place the chapatti flour in a big bowl; add half of the 120ml (4 fl oz) of water and mix well. Continue adding small amounts of water at a time and mixing well until a soft, medium dough is

formed. Divide this dough into roughly eight equal parts. Shape
these parts into round balls.

7. Sprinkle some dry flour onto the balls, and roll each ball into a
13cm (5 in) diameter round shape. Place 4 teaspoonfuls of the
mung bean filling in the middle of one half of the rolled chapatti.
Lift the other half to cover the filling completely and squeeze the
edges together, thus making a semi-circle shape with the filling in
the middle. Lift it carefully and place it on one side. Repeat this
with all the eight balls. These filled balls are called kachoris.

8. Heat the 600ml (1 pt) of oil to a high temperature, in a deep
frying pan or wok. Now add two kachoris at a time and fry each side
of the kachori until it is golden brown. This will usually take about
3–4 minutes for each side. Fry all the kachoris in this way.

9. Serve the kachoris while they are hot.

3

Bateta Chops, 63
Beef Kebabs, 61
Beef Tikka, 67
Chicken Tikka, 66
Hondwo, 64
Kadhi, 56
Lamb Kebabs with Salad, 62
Lamb Tikka, 68
Pork Tikka, 65
Spare Ribs in Tomato, 60
Spicy Lentil Soup, 55
Tandoori Chicken, 58
Tandoori Fish with Salad, 59
Tandoori Spare Rib Pork Chops with Salad, 57
Tomato Soup, 54

Savoury Starters: II

TOMATO SOUP

Indian tomato soup is a heavily spiced version of English tomato soup. It is one of the few vegetarian starters in Indian cookery and is a very light and thin soup. Like all soups, it can be served with bread or a roll.

Cooking and preparation time: 20 minutes   *Serves:* 4

450g (1 lb) ripe tomatoes
30ml (1 fl oz) cooking oil
6 whole cloves
½ tsp black mustard seeds
½ tsp asafoetida
1 tsp salt
1 tsp turmeric powder
1 tsp chilli powder
2 tsp sugar
450ml (15 fl oz) water

1. Wash all the tomatoes and cut them into very small pieces.
2. Heat the oil in a pan and add the cloves, whole black mustard seeds and asafoetida. Fry for a few seconds.
3. Add the tomatoes, salt, turmeric powder, chilli powder and the sugar. Reduce the heat, cover the pan and simmer gently for about 7 minutes.
4. Now add the water, mix well and bring to the boil. Allow it to simmer for a further 10 minutes.
5. Transfer the soup to a soup bowl; remove the cloves with a spoon and serve while hot.

SPICY LENTIL SOUP

This lentil soup can be served either on its own, as a soup, or as a side dish with a dry vegetable or fish sak, chapattis and rice.

Cooking and preparation time: 70 minutes　　　　　　　*Serves:* 4

85g (3 oz) lentils, washed and soaked for at least 30 minutes
1 tbsp oil
1 tsp black mustard seeds
3 cloves
4 black peppercorns
2–3 curry leaves
150g (5 oz) tomatoes, peeled and chopped
1 tsp crushed garlic
¼ tsp sugar
1 whole green chilli, chopped
⅛ tsp turmeric powder
¼ tsp red chilli powder
salt to taste
water as required
handful of finely chopped fresh coriander for garnish

1. Wash and soak the lentils for at least 30 minutes or overnight for best results. Drain.
2. Heat the oil in a saucepan and turn the heat to low.
3. Add the mustard seeds, cloves, peppercorns and curry leaves.
4. When the mustard seeds start to pop, add the lentils and the rest of the ingredients (*except* the coriander), adding water according to the 'soup' consistency you require.
5. Bring to the boil, lower the heat, cover and simmer for at least 40 minutes, until the lentils are mushy.
6. Liquidise or whisk the soup and garnish with coriander before serving.

Note: wash hands thoroughly after handling chillies. Mustard seeds pop, so keep the heat on low and take care when cooking them.

KADHI

When serving this hot yoghurt soup it is necessary to include a pulse dish in the meal to provide the protein. If a vegetable dish is also being served then a plain dhal will be sufficient.

Cooking and preparation time: 10–15 minutes   *Serves:* 4

500ml (1 pt) natural yoghurt
300ml (½ pt) water
2 tbsp gram flour
2 green chillies
1cm (½ in) root ginger
1½ tsp cumin seeds
1 tsp salt
1 tsp granulated sugar
1 tbsp ghee
5 curry leaves
1 tbsp green coriander, chopped

1. Put the yoghurt and water in a bowl, add the gram flour and whisk vigorously for 1 minute.
2. Mince the chillies and root ginger and add to the bowl (remembering to wash your hands after handling the chillies).
3. Crush one teaspoon of the cumin seeds and add to the bowl with the salt and sugar. Mix well together, taste and adjust seasoning as required.
4. Heat the ghee in a small pan, add the remaining cumin and sizzle for a few seconds.
5. Remove from the heat, add the curry leaves and pour into the yoghurt mixture.
6. Add the green coriander and leave in a cool place until ready to serve.
7. To serve, bring the Kadhi up to the boil, stirring continuously, and serve immediately.

TANDOORI SPARE RIB PORK CHOPS WITH SALAD

This is usually served as a mild starter. It can be used as a main dish, served with pilau rice. During summer days, it makes an excellent addition to salad, instead of ham or cold chicken. For this recipe you can either buy small, about 7.5cm (3 in) long pork chops or get your butcher to cut large chops into halves. You will require a liquidiser for this recipe.

Cooking and preparation time: 5 hours 30 minutes   *Serves:* 4

90ml (3 fl oz) plain yoghurt
1 tsp salt
1 tsp turmeric powder
2 tsp tomato purée
2 tsp tandoori masala
55g (2 oz) fresh garlic, peeled
½ tsp chilli powder
55g (2 oz) fresh ginger, peeled
4 green chillies
5–6 drops red food colouring
900g (2 lb) small spare rib pork chops
60ml (2 fl oz) cooking oil

For salad
85g (3 oz) cucumber slices
1 small onion, sliced
1 large tomato, sliced
115g (4 oz) radish, sliced
1 lettuce
1 lemon, sliced

1. Place the yoghurt, salt, turmeric powder, tomato purée, tandoori masala, garlic, chilli powder, ginger, green chillies and red colouring into a liquidiser and blend into a liquid.
2. Place the pork pieces in a large bowl, and pour the contents of the liquidiser over the pieces. Allow the meat to marinate in the mixture for the next 4 hours.
3. Place a wire rack in a baking tray. (The wire stand in the grill tray is very useful for this.)

(continued overleaf)

4. Remove all the pork pieces from the mixture and place them on the wire rack.

5. Spread the oil evenly over all the pork pieces.

6. Cook at 190°C (375°F), gas mark 5, on the middle shelf of a preheated oven, for about 45 minutes. Turn the pork pieces, remove all the excess liquid from the tray, and cook for a further 45 minutes. The excess liquid should be thrown away.

7. Take a large serving dish. Arrange the salad and lemon around the edge, and place the pork pieces in the middle of the salad.

8. Serve while the chops are still hot.

TANDOORI CHICKEN

This is a mild chicken starter. It can be served cold or hot and is very useful for picnics. You will require a liquidiser or blender for this recipe.

Cooking and preparation time: 6 hours   *Serves:* 4

900g (2 lb) chicken pieces
90ml (3 fl oz) plain yoghurt
5–6 drops of red food colouring
1 tsp salt
1 tsp turmeric powder
3 tsp tomato purée
2 tsp tandoori masala
55g (2 oz) fresh garlic, peeled
55g (2 oz) fresh ginger, peeled
5 green chillies
60ml (2 fl oz) cooking oil

1. Remove the skin from the chicken pieces. Place these pieces in a large pan.

2. Mix the yoghurt, food colouring, salt, turmeric powder, tomato purée, tandoori masala, garlic, ginger, and green chillies in a liquidiser and blend into a liquid. Pour this liquid over the chicken pieces.

3. Leave the mixture to marinate for 4–6 hours.
4. Place a wire rack in a baking tray. (The wire stand in the grill tray is very useful for this.) Remove the chicken pieces from the mixture and arrange them on the wire rack. Spread the cooking oil evenly on the chicken.
5. Cook at 190°C (375°F), gas mark 5, on the middle shelf of a preheated oven, for about 30 minutes. Remove all the excess liquid and carry on cooking for another 20 minutes. Remove any further excess liquid, turn the chicken pieces and cook for a further 30 minutes. All the excess liquid should be thrown away.
6. Place chicken in serving dish.

TANDOORI FISH WITH SALAD

This is an excellent mild starter for a special occasion. You will require a liquidiser or blender for this recipe.

Cooking and preparation time: 2 hours 45 minutes   *Serves:* 4

120ml (4 fl oz) plain yoghurt
1 tsp salt
1 tsp turmeric powder
2 tsp tomato purée
2 tsp tandoori masala
25g (1 oz) fresh garlic, peeled
25g (1 oz) fresh ginger, peeled
5–6 drops red food colouring
4 green chillies
675g (1½ lb) cod fish, cut into 10cm (4 in) long pieces
60ml (2 fl oz) cooking oil

For salad
115g (4 oz) cucumber slices
1 onion, sliced
2 tomatoes, sliced
115g (4 oz) sliced radish
fresh lettuce
1 lemon, sliced

(continued overleaf)

1. Place the yoghurt, salt, turmeric powder, tomato purée, tandoori masala, garlic, ginger, food colouring and green chillies into a liquidiser and blend into a liquid.
2. Place the fish pieces in a large pan. Pour the blended liquid over the fish and let the mixture marinate for about 2 hours.
3. Place a wire rack in a baking tray. (The wire stand in the grill tray is very useful for this.)
4. Remove all the fish pieces from the pan and place them on the wire rack.
5. Spread the oil evenly on the fish pieces.
6. Cook at 190°C (375°F), gas mark 5, on the middle shelf of a preheated oven for about 35 minutes.
7. Arrange the salad and lemon around the sides of a large serving dish and place the fish in the centre.
8. Serve while the fish is hot.

SPARE RIBS IN TOMATO

If you are fond of pork and want to try something new on the family or friends, then this dish is extremely useful. These spare ribs can be served with salad or rice. For this recipe you can either buy small spare ribs or get your butcher to cut large ribs into halves. This recipe needs a microwave oven and a deep frying pan or wok.

Cooking and preparation time: 40 minutes   *Serves:* 4

600ml (1 pt) cooking oil for frying
900g (2 lb) small spare ribs
2 tsp tomato purée
2 tsp tomato ketchup
1 tsp garlic powder
4 tsp soy sauce
90ml (3 fl oz) water

1. Heat the oil to a high temperature in a wok or deep frying pan and then deep fry the ribs until they are golden brown. This will usually take about 15–20 minutes.

2. Transfer the fried meat into a 25cm (10 in) pyrex or microwave dish.
3. Mix the tomato purée, tomato ketchup, garlic powder, soy sauce and water together and pour the mixture on top of the ribs. Place the dish in a microwave oven and cook for 10 minutes at full power.
4. Serve while hot.

BEEF KEBABS

The word *kebab* has a different meaning in Indian cookery. Indian kebabs are like burgers and are made of mince mixed with spices, and are usually served as starters. They also make excellent snacks for high teas, parties and barbecues. A special mixture of minced meat and spices makes this a mouth-watering dish! It can be served with a wedge of lemon and salad.

Cooking and preparation time: 1 hour 30 minutes   *Serves:* 4–6

510g (1 lb 2 oz) minced beef
2 medium sized onions, coarsely grated or finely sliced
4 slices bread, crumbled
4 green chillies, finely chopped
handful of fresh coriander, finely chopped
4 tsp ginger, grated
4 tsp garlic, crushed
2 tsp garam masala
1 large egg
juice of ½ lemon
salt to taste
oil for deep frying

1. Mix together all the ingredients (*except* the oil) and marinate for at least 1 hour.
2. Roll into small balls (kebabs), deep fry until golden brown and drain on kitchen roll paper. Alternatively, cook under a hot grill, turning frequently.

Note: wash hands thoroughly after handling chillies.

LAMB KEBABS WITH SALAD

Lamb kebabs are made of minced lamb mixed with spices, and are usually served as a starter. They can also be served at parties or with a glass of wine, as a snack to accompany the drink. For this recipe you need a liquidiser.

Cooking and preparation time: 1 hour 35 minutes   *Serves:* 4

25g (1 oz) fresh garlic, peeled
25g (1 oz) fresh ginger, peeled
4 green chillies
450g (1 lb) minced lamb
1 large onion, finely chopped
1 tsp salt
2 tsp tandoori masala
½ tsp chilli powder
1 tsp cumin seeds
3 tsp tomato purée

For salad
Fresh crispy lettuce
85g (3 oz) cucumber, sliced
1 small onion, sliced
2 tomatoes, sliced
1 lemon, sliced

1. Process the garlic, fresh ginger and green chillies in a liquidiser until finely chopped.
2. Mix the contents of the liquidiser, mince, onion, salt, tandoori masala, chilli powder, cumin seeds and tomato purée in a large mixing bowl. Mix everything together well.
3. Divide the mixture into roughly eight equal portions. Shape each of these portions into sausage type shapes (the kebabs).
4. Place these kebabs on the wire stand of a grill pan and cook under a hot grill for about 25 minutes turning the sides of the kebabs every 5–7 minutes. Take extreme care when turning the sides so as not to break the kebabs.
5. Arrange the salad on one side of a serving dish, and arrange the cooked kebabs on the other side of the dish.
6. Serve while hot.

BATETA CHOPS

A spicy mixture of minced meat folded into a pocket of mashed potato and fried until golden brown. Serve as a starter with a lemon wedge, salad and/or tamarind.

Cooking and preparation time: 1 hour   *Serves:* 6

250g (9 oz) mince
4 tsp garlic, crushed
4 tsp ginger, grated
salt to taste
1 tsp garam masala
·2 medium sized onions, finely chopped
handful of coriander leaves, chopped
4 green chillies, finely sliced
1kg (2 lb 2 oz) potatoes, peeled, boiled and mashed
oil for frying

For coating
2 eggs
chilli powder to taste (optional)
breadcrumbs or semolina

1. Dry cook the meat, add the garlic, ginger and salt.
2. Remove from the heat, add the garam masala, onions, coriander and chillies.
3. Take a handful of mashed potato and make a 'well' in the middle, fill with the meat mixture and roll into cakes (i.e. slightly flattened balls).
4. Whip the eggs and add some chilli powder if wanted.
5. Dip the cakes in the egg, then coat with breadcrumbs or semolina and fry until golden brown.
6. Drain on kitchen roll paper.

Note: wash hands thoroughly after handling chillies.

HONDWO

This is a vegetarian savoury cake, full of rich flavours and very delicious. Serve hot or cold with yoghurt or tamarind.

Cooking and preparation time: 3 hours 30 minutes   *Serves:* 6

200g (7 oz) Hondwo flour (from Asian stores)
115g (4 oz) rice flour
150g (5 oz) plain yoghurt
4 tsp garlic, crushed
3 tsp ginger, grated
55g (2 oz) semolina
55g (2 oz) gram flour
4 green chillies, finely chopped
handful coriander leaves, finely chopped
1 tsp sugar
1 small carrot, coarsely grated
1 small potato, coarsely grated
1 medium sized onion, finely chopped
1 tbsp peas
handful cabbage, finely shredded
1–2 tbsp lemon juice
salt to taste
3 tbsp oil
1 tsp cumin seeds
2 tsp black mustard seeds
6 curry leaves
1 tsp Eno's fruit salt (available from chemists)
2 tsp sesame seeds

1. Put all the ingredients into a bowl *except* for the oil, cumin and mustard seeds, curry leaves, Eno's salt and sesame seeds.
2. Add enough hot water to mix into a thick paste, then allow to stand overnight or at least for 2 hours.
3. Heat the oil, add the cumin and mustard seeds and curry leaves.
4. When the seeds start to pop, pour into the mixture and stir.
5. Stir in the Eno's salt.
6. Pour the mixture into a well-greased baking tin and place in a pre-heated oven at 190°C (375°F), gas mark 5.
7. After 30 minutes, sprinkle the top with the sesame seeds.
8. Cook for another 40 minutes or until the top appears golden brown and when a skewer is inserted it comes out clean.

Note: wash hands thoroughly after handling chillies.

PORK TIKKA

All tikka dishes make very good starters and snacks. As a starter these pork pieces, marinated and cooked in yoghurt, are usually served with a salad. For this recipe you will need a liquidiser.

Cooking and preparation time: 8 hours 50 minutes   *Serves:* 4

25g (1 oz) fresh garlic, peeled
25g (1 oz) fresh ginger, peeled
4 green chillies
180ml (6 fl oz) fresh natural yoghurt
2 tsp soy sauce
1 tsp salt
2 tsp tomato purée
1 tsp turmeric powder
1 tsp chilli powder
1 tsp red food colouring
15ml (½ fl oz) lemon juice
340g (12 oz) pork steak
60ml (2 fl oz) cooking oil
120ml (4 fl oz) water

1. Mix the garlic, ginger, chillies, yoghurt, soy sauce, salt, tomato purée, turmeric powder, chilli powder, red food colouring and lemon juice in a liquidiser and blend it into a liquid.
2. Cut the pork steak into small 1cm (½ in) cubes.
3. Place the pork pieces in a large pan and then pour the blended mixture on the pork pieces.
4. Leave the mixture to marinate for about 8 hours.
5. Heat the oil in a large pan to a high temperature and then add the pork with all its spiced liquid. Stir continuously and cook for about 10 minutes.
6. Add the water, cover the pan, lower the heat and let it simmer for about 35 minutes, stirring every 5–7 minutes.
7. Remove the cover of the pan, raise the heat and let the water evaporate, leaving a rather dry pork tikka. This will usually take about 3–4 minutes.
8. Serve hot, with salad or on its own.

CHICKEN TIKKA

Like all tikka dishes these chicken pieces, marinated and cooked in yoghurt, make very good starters and snacks and are usually served with a salad. For this recipe you need a liquidiser and a sharp knife.

Cooking and preparation time: 8 hours 40 minutes   *Serves:* 4

25g (1 oz) fresh garlic, peeled
25g (1 oz) fresh ginger, peeled
4 green chillies
180ml (6 fl oz) fresh natural yoghurt
2 tsp soy sauce
1 tsp salt
2 tsp tomato purée
1 tsp turmeric powder
1 tsp chilli powder
1 tsp red food colouring
15ml (½ fl oz) lemon juice
675g (1½ lb) chicken pieces
60ml (2 fl oz) cooking oil
60ml (2 fl oz) water

1. Place the garlic, ginger, chillies, yoghurt, soy sauce, salt, tomato purée, turmeric powder, chilli powder, red colouring and lemon juice in a liquidiser and blend into a liquid.
2. Remove the skin from the chicken pieces and chop into about 2.5cm (1 in) long pieces.
3. Place the chicken pieces in a large pan and pour over the blended mixture.
4. Leave this mixture to marinate for about 8 hours.
5. Heat the oil in a large pan to a high temperature and then add the chicken with all its spiced liquid. Stir continuously and cook for about 10 minutes.
6. Now add the water, cover the pan, lower the heat and let it simmer for about 25 minutes, stirring every 5–7 minutes.
7. Now remove the cover of the pan, raise the heat and let the water evaporate, leaving a rather dry chicken dish. This will usually take about 3–4 minutes.
8. Serve hot, with salad or on its own.

BEEF TIKKA

Beef tikka (beef pieces, marinated and cooked in yoghurt) also makes a very good starter or a snack served with a salad. For this recipe you need a liquidiser.

Cooking and preparation time: 9 hours   *Serves:* 4

25g (1 oz) fresh garlic, peeled
25g (1 oz) fresh ginger, peeled
4 green chillies
180ml (6 fl oz) fresh natural yoghurt
2 tsp soy sauce
1 tsp salt
2 tsp tomato purée
1 tsp turmeric powder
1 tsp chilli powder
1 tsp red food colouring
15ml (½ fl oz) lemon juice
340g (12 oz) beef steak
60ml (2 fl oz) cooking oil
180ml (6 fl oz) water

1. Place the garlic, ginger, chillies, yoghurt, soy sauce, salt, tomato purée, turmeric powder, chilli powder, red colouring and lemon juice in a liquidiser and blend into a liquid.
2. Cut the beef steak into small, 1cm (½ in) cubes.
3. Place the beef pieces in a large pan, and then pour the blended mixture on to the beef pieces.
4. Leave this mixture to marinate for about 8 hours.
5. Heat the oil in a large pan to a high temperature, and then add the beef with all its spiced liquid. Stir continuously, and cook for about 10 minutes.
6. Add the water, cover the pan, lower the heat and let it simmer for about 45 minutes, stirring every 5–7 minutes.
7. Remove the cover of the pan, raise the heat and let the water evaporate, leaving a rather dry beef dish. This will usually take about 3–4 minutes.
8. Serve hot, with salad or on its own.

LAMB TIKKA

Lamb pieces, marinated and cooked in yoghurt, make another tikka dish that is a very good starter or snack usually served with a salad. For this recipe you need a liquidiser.

Cooking and preparation time: 9 hours   *Serves:* 4

25g (1 oz) fresh garlic, peeled
25g (1 oz) fresh ginger, peeled
4 green chillies
180ml (6 fl oz) fresh natural yoghurt
2 tsp soy sauce
1 tsp salt
2 tsp tomato purée
1 tsp turmeric powder
1 tsp chilli powder
1 tsp red food colouring
15ml (½ fl oz) lemon juice
340g (12 oz) diced lamb
60ml (2 fl oz) cooking oil
150ml (5 fl oz) water

1. Place the garlic, ginger, chillies, yoghurt, soy sauce, salt, tomato purée, turmeric powder, chilli powder, red colouring and lemon juice in a liquidiser and blend into a liquid.
2. Place the lamb pieces in a large pan, and pour the blended mixture on to the lamb pieces.
3. Leave this mixture to marinate for about 8 hours.
4. Heat the oil in a large pan to a high temperature and then add the lamb with all its spiced liquid. Stir continuously, and cook for about 10 minutes.
5. Add the water, cover the pan, lower the heat and let it simmer for about 40 minutes, stirring every 5–7 minutes.
6. Remove the cover of the pan, raise the heat and let the water evaporate, leaving a rather dry lamb dish. This will usually take about 3–4 minutes.
7. Serve hot, with salad or on its own.

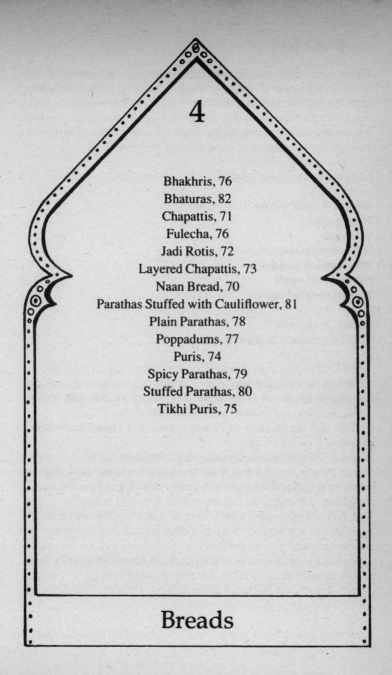

4

Breads

NAAN BREAD

This is made with very simple, healthy ingredients and is delicious when freshly made! You can be ambitious and experiment by adding other ingredients such as garlic, very finely chopped onion or whole cumin seeds. Serve with any of the saks (spicy or curried vegetable dishes with little or no sauce) or stuffed, with kebabs, finely sliced cabbage, onion, cucumber and a squeeze of lemon juice.

Cooking and preparation time: 1 hour 30 minutes   *Serves:* 4–6

450g (1 lb) plain flour
1 tsp sugar
½ tsp salt
½ tsp bicarbonate of soda
1 tsp baking powder
2 tbsp dried yeast
2–3 tbsp plain yoghurt
1 egg
125ml (¼ pt) milk
50g (2 oz) butter or margarine

1. Mix all the dry ingredients with the yeast, yoghurt and egg.
2. Warm the milk and add to the dry mixture a little at a time until the dough forms. (It is possible that not all of the milk will be required: the dough should be firm and not soggy.)
3. Turn the dough onto a floured surface and knead for at least 5 minutes.
4. Put in a lightly floured bowl, cover with a wet cloth and leave in a warm place to rise for at least 40 minutes or until the dough has doubled in size and springs back easily when lightly pressed.
5. Return the dough to a floured surface and knead again. Divide into six or eight equal size balls and allow to rise for about 20 minutes in a warm place until they have almost doubled in size and spring back easily when pressed.
6. Roll out the balls with a rolling pin on a floured surface or flatten in the palms of your hands to about 5mm (¼ in) thick.
7. Brush with melted butter and cook under a hot grill until golden brown, and repeat on the other side.

Note: the grill should not be too hot to ensure that the naan is allowed to cook before it turns golden brown.

CHAPATTIS

Of all the breads, chapattis, also called rotis, are probably eaten most often. They can be served with most curries and they are especially good with sak dishes. As they are rolled thinly and roasted, rather than fried, they are lighter and easier to digest. If you are new to chapatti making, use tongs to turn your chapattis over when cooking them on the wire rack, which should be set over very high heat. Both gas and electric cookers are suitable for making chapattis.

Cooking and preparation time: 11-17 minutes   *Serves:* 4–6

450g (1 lb) chapatti flour
2 tbsp oil
hot water
ghee (page 246) for spreading
plain flour for rolling

1. Put the chapatti flour into a bowl, add the oil and mix lightly. Add enough hot water to form a soft dough. If the dough is sticky, add a teaspoon of melted ghee to the bowl and continue to knead.
2. Divide the dough into walnut-sized pieces. Set your griddle on a medium setting. If you don't have a griddle, then a heavy frying pan or a tavi will do. You will also need a wire rack set on an open flame or a very hot radiant ring.
3. Flatten a piece of dough between the palms of your hands and dip it in the plain flour. Now roll out to a thin round chapatti, approximately 15cm (6 in) in diameter.
4. Cook for 1 minute on the griddle (or frying pan), turning once. Do not add any oil or butter to the frying pan as chapattis are cooked dry.
5. Turn onto the wire rack over high heat. The chapatti should, at this stage, bubble up into a round balloon. Turn quickly to avoid burning. When lightly browned on both sides, put on a warm plate and spread with ghee. Pile the chapattis on top of each other as you make them. Do not worry if your chapattis won't bubble up completely. They will be quite acceptable if you cook them on both sides without burning them.

JADI ROTIS

These thick chapattis are very simple to make and are good to serve with curries and pulses. Serve them hot or cold or pack them for a picnic with Split Moong Dhal (page 207) and a salad.

Cooking and preparation time: 20–30 minutes   *Serves:* 4–6

450g (1 lb) chapatti flour
1 tsp salt
3 tbsp cooking oil
hot water
3–4 tbsp melted ghee (page 246) for brushing
plain flour for dusting

1. Put the chapatti flour and salt into a large bowl, add the oil and rub in. Add enough hot water to form a soft, pliable dough. Divide the dough into large tangerine-sized balls.
2. Heat a tavi or a non-stick frying pan over a medium heat. Also set a wire rack over a high heat. (If you are using gas you can turn it up and down when required.)
3. Flatten each ball between the palms of your hands, coat in plain flour and roll out to a 5cm (2 in) disc.
4. Brush with a little melted ghee. Sprinkle on some plain flour and bring up the edges to enclose the ghee and plain flour and form back into a ball.
5. Flatten again between your palms and roll out on a floured board to 15cm (6 in) in diameter.
6. Cook on the heated tavi or frying pan for 1 minute, turning once after 20–30 seconds. Turn onto the wire rack over the high heat and cook, turning quickly until bubbled up and lightly browned.
7. Repeat this process with the rest of the balls. Brush melted ghee over each roti (chapatti) as it cooks and stack them up.

LAYERED CHAPATTIS

These chapattis are ideal to serve with curries and pulse dishes, and can be presented hot or cold, either on the side or with the curry or pulse dish spooned over it. In this way they can be served as a first course or a main course.

Cooking and preparation time: 32–38 minutes   *Serves:* 6

450g (1 lb) chapatti flour
1 tsp salt
2 tbsp cooking oil
hot water
2–3 tbsp melted ghee for brushing (page 246)
plain flour for dusting

1. Put the chapatti flour and the salt in a large bowl, add the oil and rub in with the fingertips. Add enough hot water to form a pliable dough. Divide the dough into large tangerine-sized balls. Roll each ball out on a floured board to about 15cm (6 in) in diameter. Brush melted ghee over the round shape and dust with a little plain flour. Fold in half and brush with melted ghee and dust with plain flour. Fold in half twice more, each time brushing with ghee and dusting with flour. You should end up with a rough triangular shape. Do the same with the rest of the balls.
2. Now heat a tavi or a non-stick frying pan over a low to medium heat. Carefully flatten each layered piece of dough on a floured board to approximately 5mm (¼ in) in thickness. Try and keep the basic shape triangular as you roll out.
3. Cook each chapatti slowly on the tavi or frying pan, turning frequently, until it has bubbled up and is marked with golden spots all over.
4. Brush a little ghee on the cooked chapatti and cool on a wire rack. Make all the chapattis in this way.

PURIS

Puris are a type of chapatti but are much smaller, deep fried and different in taste. These will keep for several days in an airtight container. Serve with Kheer (page 250) or for breakfast with fried eggs or Murbo (page 240).

Cooking and preparation time: 50 minutes   *Serves:* 6

200g (7 oz) plain flour
200g (7 oz) chapatti flour
3 tbsp oil
¼ tsp salt
¼ tsp turmeric powder
hot water
oil for deep frying

1. Mix together all the ingredients (*except* the oil for frying), adding just enough hot water to bind into a dough.
2. Heat the oil for frying.
3. Divide the dough into equal sized balls, the size of walnuts.
4. Roll out into small, thin chapatti shapes.
5. Immerse in the hot oil and deep fry, until both sides are golden brown.

TIKHI PURIS

These hot and spicy fried breads go very well served with a cup of Gujarati-style Tea (page 276) and some fried poppadums. They are also ideal to take on picnics. You will need a wok or deep frying pan for this recipe.

Cooking and preparation time: 40–50 minutes   *Serves:* 6–8

450g (1 lb) chapatti flour
4 tbsp cooking oil
3 cloves garlic
4 green chillies
1 tsp crushed cumin seeds
1 tsp ground turmeric
1½ tsp salt
warm water
oil for deep frying

1. Put the chapatti flour in a large bowl, add the oil and rub into the flour with the fingertips. Mince the garlic and chillies together and add to the flour with the crushed cumin, turmeric and salt. Mix well, then add enough warm water to form a soft dough. (Wash hands thoroughly after handling the chillies.)
2. Divide the dough into little balls the size of walnuts. Roll each ball out to a 7.5cm (3 in) diameter and spread the rolled discs on a clean tea towel.
3. Heat the oil over a medium heat. When a little piece of the dough is dropped into the oil and it rises to the surface almost immediately, the oil is ready for frying.
4. Lower a rolled out disc into the hot oil, wait until it rises to the surface then turn it over. Cook for 10–15 seconds or until lightly browned.
5. Remove from the oil and drain on absorbent kitchen roll paper. Repeat this process until all the puris are cooked.

FULECHA

This fried bread is ideal to serve at buffet parties. Make a day in advance and store in an airtight container to keep soft. Serve a variety of different vegetable and pulse dishes which the guests can spoon over their fulecha. They're also good to serve with a curry.

Cooking and preparation time: 25–30 minutes   *Serves:* 6–8

450g (1 lb) chapatti flour
3 tbsp oil
1 tsp salt
2 tbsp natural yoghurt
hot water
oil for deep frying

1. Use the above ingredients to form a soft dough and divide into four equal parts.
2. Roll out on a lightly floured board to about 3mm (⅛ in) thickness.
3. Cut into large diamond shapes and deep fry in hot oil until puffed up and lightly browned (approximately 1 minute for each batch).

BHAKHRIS

A freshly cooked bhakhri (or shallow fried bread) is quite delicious eaten on its own. It is often served with Split Pea Dahl (see page 204). Unlike chapattis, you do not stack bhakhris. They should be spread out on a wire rack to cool. This helps to keep them crisp until you are ready to serve. In an Indian home, bhakhris are sometimes served instead of chapattis when entertaining guests.

Cooking and preparation time: 12–22 minutes   *Serves:* 6–8

6 tbsp melted ghee (page 246)
450g (1 lb) chapatti flour
warm water
oil for frying

1. Rub the ghee into the flour, then use enough warm water to make a firm dough. Divide the dough into walnut-sized pieces.

2. Heat a heavy frying pan or tavi over a medium heat.

3. Roll out the bhakhri dough thick and small – approximately 7.5cm (3 in) in diameter.

4. Cook on both sides in the frying pan without oil. Then add a teaspoon of oil and allow the bhakhri to bubble up. Turn and cook the other side. Bhakhris should be golden brown and crisp on the outside.

Variation: to make sweet bhakhris, dissolve 4 tbsp of sugar in the water which is added to make the dough.

POPPADUMS

Poppadums come in three main varieties – made from rice flour, mung bean flour or black matape bean flour. Within these three varieties there are a number of sub-varieties, each having different quantities of spices mixed in them. When you buy poppadums, do check on whether they are hot or mild. It may be an idea to try different types to find out which you prefer. It is very difficult to recommend one particular variety, as it very much depends on individual taste.

Poppadums can be deep fried (one at a time, in about 1 litre (2 pt) of cooking oil heated to a high temperature), or grilled, like toast. It takes about half a minute to grill each side, but the deep fry method is much quicker, taking literally seconds, once the oil is heated.

It is normally recommended that rice poppadums should be deep fried, but bean flour poppadums taste good done either way. In most restaurants, only fried poppadums are served.

PLAIN PARATHAS

This bread is thick and round and quite substantial so allow one or two per person, according to their appetite. Serve these with any of the sak dishes and Spicy Yoghurt Chutney (page 238) for a delicious main course at a dinner party. They are also good with curries.

Cooking and preparation time: 23–34 minutes   *Serves:* 4–6

3 tbsp oil
450g (1 lb) chapatti flour
1 tbsp natural yoghurt
warm water
125g (4 oz) plain flour (for dipping, sprinkling and rolling)
slightly salted butter, softened

1. Mix the oil into the flour. Make a hole in the middle, add the yoghurt and enough warm water to make a soft dough.
2. Divide the dough into small tangerine-sized pieces, flatten each piece between the palms of your hands and dip in the flour. Roll out one at a time into a round circle.
3. Spread lightly with softened butter and sprinkle with plain flour. Fold in half and repeat the process. Fold into a quarter and spread again.
4. Sprinkle plain flour on the quartered piece and gather up the three corners and roll lightly between the palms to a flattened ball.
5. Roll out each paratha on a floured board into a thick round shape – approximately 12cm (5 in) in diameter. Cook slowly on the griddle or a heavy frying pan over a medium heat.
6. Turn several times until the paratha is lightly browned on both sides.

SPICY PARATHAS

An excellent type of chapatti, with a combination of flavours. Serve hot with saks, pickles or for breakfast with fried eggs, jam or anything that takes your fancy!

Cooking and preparation time: 1 hour   *Serves:* 6

450g (1 lb) chapatti flour
¼ tsp salt
3 tbsp oil
¼ tsp turmeric powder
¼ tsp chilli powder
handful of coriander and fenugreek leaves, chopped
hot water
oil for frying

1. Mix together all the ingredients (*except* for the frying oil), adding just enough hot water to bind into a dough.
2. Heat a frying pan and turn the heat down to medium.
3. Divide the dough into six equal sized balls and roll each one in the palms of your hands for 1 minute.
4. Roll out into thickened chapatti shapes.
5. Without any oil, part cook both sides in the frying pan until just brown.
6. Next, fry both sides with a drop of oil until golden.

STUFFED PARATHAS

There are several variations of this dish and once you have mastered the basic principle you will be able to experiment with many different fillings of your choice. When rolling out each paratha handle very gently to avoid having the filling ooze out. Serve hot with a pulse dish and Spicy Yoghurt Chutney (page 238) or with one of the yoghurt dishes.

Cooking and preparation time: 32 minutes   *Serves:* 4–6

225g (8 oz) chapatti flour
2 tbsp oil
warm water
3 green chillies
2.5cm (1 in) root ginger
½ bunch green coriander
2 large potatoes, boiled and mashed
1 tsp salt
1 tsp ground turmeric
1 tbsp sesame seeds
2 tbsp desiccated coconut
1 tsp granulated sugar
oil for shallow frying

1. Combine the flour, oil and enough warm water to form a soft dough.
2. Mince the chillies and ginger and chop the coriander finely. Mix with the remaining ingredients and form into walnut-sized stuffing balls. (Remember to wash your hands thoroughly after handling the chillies.)
3. Divide the dough into slightly larger balls. Make a hole in the middle of a ball of dough and place a ball of stuffing in it and bring the dough over the top to cover the stuffing.
4. Seal well and roll out on a lightly floured board into a flat round shape, approximately 12cm (5 in) in diameter.
5. Set a heavy based frying pan over medium heat and shallow fry the parathas using 1 tbsp of oil at a time. Turn the parathas and cook the other side. They should be crisp and golden on the outside.

PARATHAS STUFFED WITH CAULIFLOWER

Stuffed parathas do not need curries and they are often cooked for high teas or picnics. Cauliflower-stuffed parathas are very different and sometimes served for breakfast in the northern parts of India. For this recipe you need a large flat frying pan or tavi and a grater.

Cooking and preparation time: 1 hour   *Makes:* about 8 parathas

450g (1 lb) cauliflower
½ tsp salt
½ tsp garam masala
½ tsp chilli powder
450g (1 lb) white chapatti flour (sieved)
30ml (1 fl oz) cooking oil
210ml (7 fl oz) water
115g (4 oz) chapatti flour, for rolling
240ml (8 fl oz) cooking oil, for frying parathas

1. Cut and wash the cauliflower and then grate it.
2. Mix the cauliflower, salt, garam masala and the chilli powder. After mixing, squeeze out all the water from the grated spiced cauliflower.
3. Mix the sieved flour and the 30ml (1 fl oz) of cooking oil in a bowl and leave it for a few seconds.
4. Add water gradually to the above mixture and continue to mix well, until a medium stiff dough is formed. Leave the dough in a cool place for about 30 minutes.
5. Divide the dough into about 8 roughly equal portions and shape them into balls. Sprinkle flour onto a rolling area and roll the balls into discs about 15cm (6 in) in diameter.
6. Place two tablespoonfuls of spiced cauliflower onto the flat rolled chapatti, and sprinkle a little bit of dry flour on top. Fold the chapatti into a ball in such a way that the cauliflower is completely covered by the dough. Roll out the balls again into discs, about 17cm (7 in) in diameter.
7. Heat a tavi or flat pan to a high temperature and place the rolled paratha on the pan. Leave it for a few seconds. Now turn it over and cook the other side for a few seconds. Turn it over again and cook for a further few seconds.

(continued overleaf)

8. Now spread a teaspoonful of cooking oil on top of the cooking paratha and turn it over so that the oiled side is underneath. Spread the other side similarly with cooking oil and turn again to cook the second side. Continue cooking until both sides of the paratha are light brown. Remove the paratha from the pan and place it in a dish.
9. Cook all the parathas in this way.

BHATURAS

Bhaturas can be served with almost any curry dish, but are usually served with chick peas, and raita. They taste like very soft bread, and are served instead of chapattis or puris (deep fried chapattis). For this recipe you need a deep frying pan or wok.

Cooking and preparation time: 4 hours 40 minutes   *Serves:* 4

450g (1 lb) plain flour, sieved, for dough
1 tsp baking powder, sieved
300ml (½ pt) plain yoghurt
55g (2 oz) plain flour, for rolling
600ml (1 pt) cooking oil, for deep frying

1. Mix the flour, baking powder and yoghurt in a large mixing bowl, and make a medium soft dough. Leave the dough covered for 4 hours.
2. Divide the dough into about 12 equal parts.
3. Shape each part into a ball, flour the surface of the balls well with dry flour. Roll the balls flat into 5mm (¼ in) thick, 12–15cm (5–6 in) diameter discs.
4. Heat the oil to a high temperature in a wok or deep frying pan, and then reduce the heat. Deep fry the rolled bhatura, which will float, one at a time, for about ½ minute on each side. Drain the oil from the bhatura and place in a serving dish. Repeat this with all the bhaturas.
5. Serve hot.

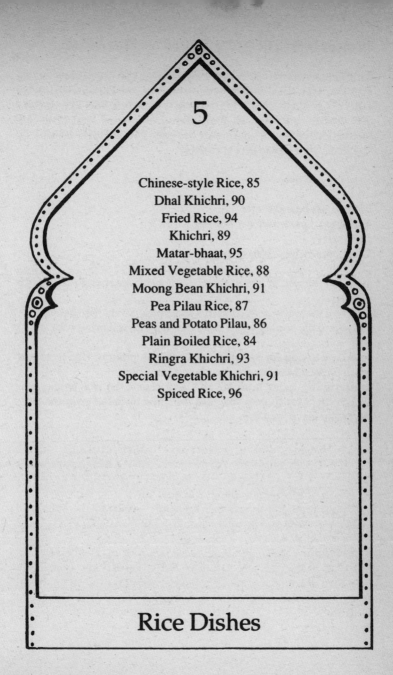

5

Rice Dishes

PLAIN BOILED RICE

This simple rice recipe is very commonly used in everyday cooking. You may use ordinary butter in this recipe if you wish, but in other recipes in this book, where ghee is called for, it is important to use it as it will make all the difference to your final dish. For instructions on how to make ghee see page 246. It is also possible to buy ghee from Indian grocery shops.

Cooking and preparation time: 20–27 minutes   *Serves:* 3–4

225g (8 oz) basmati rice
1.5 litres (3 pt) water for boiling
1 tsp salt
1 tbsp ghee (page 246) or butter

1. Wash the rice in two to three changes of water and soak for 15 minutes.
2. Bring the water to the boil in a large pan. Strain the soaking rice and add to the boiling water. Add the salt, stir and bring back to the boil.
3. Allow to boil for 5–7 minutes or until a grain of rice feels soft when pressed between the thumb and forefinger.
4. Strain the water from the rice and return the rice to the pan. Reduce the heat to very low, dot the ghee or butter over the rice, cover and leave for 1 minute.

CHINESE-STYLE RICE

A very simple dish that will utilise left-overs and, although not Indian, is nice in combination with some of the dry dishes! Serve on its own or with Tandoori Chicken (page 145).

Cooking and preparation time: 1 hour 20 minutes   *Serves:* 4–6

400g (14 oz) rice, washed and soaked for 30 minutes
salt to taste
150g (5 oz) mixed vegetables (diced carrots, green peppers, beans, etc.)
1 large onion, sliced
3 tsp garlic, crushed
5 tsp ginger, grated
2 tbsp oil
50g (2 oz) peeled prawns (optional)
50g (2 oz) cooked chicken bits (optional)
2 eggs
1 tsp tabasco sauce (or to taste)
3 tbsp soy sauce
ground black pepper to taste

1. Wash, soak and drain the rice, then boil it in fresh water, adding salt to taste, until just cooked (about 40 minutes). Drain and rinse.
2. Stir fry the vegetables with the onion, garlic and ginger and put aside.
3. Stir fry the prawns and chicken bits (if using) and put aside.
4. Scramble the eggs and put aside.
5. Put all the ingredients *except* the rice, eggs and black pepper into the fry-pan, stir and heat gently.
6. Carefully mix all the ingredients into the rice and serve.

PEAS AND POTATO PILAU

Savoury rice made with very simple ingredients. This dish could also be served as a main course with salad, raita and pickles.

Cooking and preparation time: 2 hours   *Serves:* 4–6

450g (1 lb) rice, washed and soaked for 40 minutes
3 tbsp oil
1 large onion, sliced
2 tsp cumin seeds
3 cardamom pods
2 × 2.5cm (1 in) cinnamon sticks
8 cloves
8 black peppercorns
4 tsp garlic, crushed
4 tsp ginger, grated
4 green chillies, whole or chopped
handful of coriander leaves, chopped
150g (5 oz) tomatoes, peeled or chopped
200g (7 oz) peas
6 medium sized potatoes, peeled and quartered
4–6 hard boiled eggs
250ml (½ pt) water
salt to taste
25g (1 oz) butter or margarine

1. Wash and soak the rice, then drain it.
2. Heat the oil in a large saucepan and add the onion, cumin seeds, cardamom pods, cinnamon sticks, cloves and peppercorns.
3. When the onion has softened, add the garlic, ginger, chillies and coriander and cook for 2 minutes.
4. Next, add the tomatoes, peas, potatoes, eggs, water, salt and rice and stir.
5. Bring to the boil, cover and simmer on a low heat for 40 minutes, until the rice has cooked.
6. Add the butter in blobs while the pilau is still hot.

Note: to prevent rice from going mushy, never stir while it is cooking.
Wash hands thoroughly after handling chillies.

PEA PILAU RICE

This is one of the many rice dishes usually served with any curry or split pulse dish.

Cooking and preparation time: 1 hour 30 minutes   *Serves:* 4

170g (6 oz) basmati rice
390ml (13 fl oz) water
60ml (2 fl oz) cooking oil
½ tsp cumin seeds
½ tsp black mustard seeds
½ tsp salt
½ tsp turmeric powder
½ tsp chilli powder
1 tsp tomato purée
85g (3 oz) frozen peas

1. Wash the rice like a dhal as described in the introduction (page 12).
2. Soak the rice for about 1 hour in the water.
3. Heat the oil in a pan and add the cumin and black mustard seeds. Leave to cook for a few seconds.
4. Very carefully add the soaked rice and water, salt, turmeric powder, chilli powder, tomato purée, and peas. If they are added too quickly, the mixture will spit all over the place. Bring the mixture to the boil.
5. Reduce the heat, cover the pan and let it simmer gently for about 20 minutes.
6. Transfer the contents to a serving dish, and serve while hot.

MIXED VEGETABLE RICE

This colourful dish is ideal to serve at dinner parties. Choose a pulse dish and a yoghurt dish to go with it. It is also delicious served cold at picnics. When stirring, take care not to break up the vegetables.

Cooking and preparation time: 20–30 minutes   *Serves:* 6–8

450g (1 lb) basmati rice
6 tbsp oil
3 tbsp ghee (page 246)
2.5cm (1 in) stick cinnamon
3 cloves
2 black peppercorns
1 large onion, chopped
1 large potato, cubed
2 carrots, cubed
115g (4 oz) frozen peas (defrosted)
2 tsp salt
1 tsp ground turmeric
1 tsp chilli powder
1 tbsp ground coriander
750ml (1½ pt) boiling water

1. Wash the rice and soak in warm water. Heat the oil and ghee together in a large pan. When hot, add the cinnamon, cloves, black peppercorns and onion and cook for 3 minutes.
2. Add the potato and carrots and cook, covered, over medium heat until tender.
3. Add the peas, salt, turmeric, chilli powder, coriander and cook for a further 2 minutes.
4. Drain the rice and add to the pan. Stir fry for 1 minute, reduce the heat, then add the boiling water, cover and cook until all the water is absorbed.
5. Test a grain of rice by pressing between thumb and forefinger. If it is still hard or grainy you will need to add a little more water and cook further until all the water is absorbed and the rice is soft when tested as above.

KHICHRI

This is a tasty but easy meal to serve. Kadhi and Bindi Sak (pages 56 and 164) are the ideal accompaniments. You could, of course, choose any other vegetable dish but Kadhi must always be served with it, along with a dollop of ghee (page 246).

Cooking and preparation time: 40–45 minutes   *Serves:* 6–8

170g (6 oz) split pigeon peas
340g (12 oz) American long grain rice
2 litres (4 pt) water (approximately)
1½ tsp salt
½ tsp ground turmeric
2 cloves garlic, peeled and slivered
ghee to serve (page 246)

1. Soak the split pigeon peas in hot water for 30 minutes. Wash the rice in two or three changes of water and soak for 30 minutes.
2. In a large heavy based pan bring the water to the boil. Wash and drain the split peas. Also drain the soaking water out of the rice. Add the rice and split peas to the boiling water in the pan. Bring back to the boil and stir in the salt, turmeric and slivered garlic. Boil rapidly until the mixture is cooked. The grains should be quite soft. (Do not worry too much about over cooking this dish.)
3. Empty into a sieve and drain off all the water left in the pan. Return the khichri to the pan, lower the heat to very low and simmer with the lid on for 1 minute.

DHAL KHICHRI

Another type of khichri made with a mixture of rice and lentils.
Serve with Potato Sak or Vegetable Sak (pages 176 and 171).

Cooking and preparation time: 1 hour 20 minutes   *Serves:* 4

150g (5 oz) rice } **washed and soaked for**
85g (3 oz) lentils } **at least 30 minutes**
1 tbsp oil
5 cloves
5 black peppercorns
2.5cm (1 in) cinnamon stick
1 tsp cumin seeds
1 very small onion, finely sliced
250ml (½ pt) water
½ tsp turmeric powder
2 tsp salt (or to taste)

1. Wash and soak the grains.
2. Heat the oil, add the whole spices and the onion, and cook until
the onion softens.
3. Add the grains, the water, the turmeric and salt.
4. Bring to the boil, cover and simmer on a low heat for 40 minutes
until the grains are soft to the touch.

Note: do not stir this dish when cooking or it will go mushy!

MOONG BEAN KHICHRI

Serve with a vegetable sak.

Cooking and preparation time: 1 hour 10 minutes   *Serves:* 4–6

85g (3 oz) split mung beans   } **washed and soaked**
150g (5 oz) rice   } **for at least 30 minutes**
500ml (1 pt) water
1 tsp salt (or to taste)
50g (2 oz) butter or margarine

1. Wash the grains and soak for at least half an hour.
2. Put all the ingredients in a saucepan *except* for the butter.
3. Bring to the boil, cover and simmer for 40 minutes until cooked to a very mushy appearance. (It may be necessary to add more water during cooking if the mixture becomes too dry.)
4. Finally, add the butter and stir in before serving.

SPECIAL VEGETABLE KHICHRI

This wonderful spicy rice is a meal in its own right. It is often served at garden parties and fêtes. You could serve it with Kadhi (page 56) or a yoghurt dish if you wished, or perhaps a little Green Mango Chutney (page 239) and poppadums.

Cooking and preparation time: 50–55 minutes   *Serves:* 6–8

340g (12 oz) American long grain rice
2 carrots
1 small potato
½ large onion
½ large aubergine
50g (2 oz) frozen peas
3 cloves garlic
2 green chillies

(continued overleaf)

4 tbsp cooking oil
4 tbsp ghee (page 246)
2 sticks of cinnamon
6 cloves
4 cardamom pods
6 black peppercorns
2 tsp salt
1 tsp ground turmeric
boiling water

1. Wash the rice in several changes of water and then leave soaking in some fresh water for 30 minutes.
2. Meanwhile, peel the carrots and potato and chop finely. Peel and chop the onion finely. Wash and cut the aubergine into 1.5cm (½ in) cubes. Soak the peas in warm water to defrost. Peel and crush the garlic and chop the chillies very finely.
3. In a large heavy based pan, heat the oil and ghee together. Add the cinnamon sticks, cloves, cardamoms and black peppercorns. Throw in the chopped carrots, stir and cover the pan. Reduce the heat to medium and cook for 2 minutes.
4. Add the chopped onion and potato. Stir well and cook, covered, for 3 minutes.
5. Now add the cubed aubergine, salt and turmeric. Stir carefully so as not to break up the vegetables and allow to cook for a further 3 minutes with the lid on.
6. Drain the peas and add to the pan along with the crushed garlic and the finely chopped chillies. Mix well and cook, uncovered, for 1 minute.
7. Add the drained rice and stir fry gently for 2 minutes. It is very important to stir gently at this stage as the soaked rice will break easily. Now add enough boiling water to cover and rise to about 2.5cm (1 in) above the contents of the pan.
8. Cover tightly and simmer gently for the next 10 minutes. Stir occasionally until the rice is cooked and all the water is absorbed. Add a little more hot water if the contents of the pan seem to be going too dry.

RINGRA KHICHRI

An excellent, healthy combination of simple ingredients such as aubergines and mung beans makes up this tasty dish. Serve as an accompaniment with a main course of Vegetable Sak (page 171).

Cooking and preparation time: 1 hour   *Serves:* 4–6

2 tbsp oil
3 cloves
3 black peppercorns
2.5cm (1 in) cinnamon stick
3 cardamom pods, opened
1 tsp cumin seeds
1 small onion, finely sliced
2 tsp crushed garlic
85g (3 oz) tomatoes, peeled and chopped
1 small aubergine, cut into 2.5cm (1 in) cubes
2 medium sized potatoes, peeled and quartered
85g (3 oz) split mung beans
150g (5 oz) rice
250ml (½ pt) water
1 tsp salt (or to taste)
50g (2 oz) butter or margarine

1. Heat the oil and add all the whole spices and the onion and fry until the onion has softened.
2. Add the garlic, fry for 2 minutes, and then add the rest of the ingredients, *except* the butter.
3. Stir, cover and simmer for 40 minutes.
4. Keep checking to ensure the mixture is not drying up, and, if necessary, add drops of water to aid the cooking and keep it moist.
5. Ten minutes before serving, add the butter in small blobs.

FRIED RICE

Fried rice can feature as a snack or at high tea, without curry or dhals. Left-over plain boiled rice can also be fried in the manner described below. For this recipe you need a large wok or deep frying pan.

Cooking and preparation time: 1 hour 30 minutes   *Serves:* 4

170g (6 oz) plain basmati rice
1500ml (2½ pt) water
60ml (2 fl oz) cooking oil
½ tsp black mustard seeds
½ tsp cumin seeds
¼ tsp asafoetida
1 small onion, finely chopped
1 small potato, chopped into very small pieces
½ tsp turmeric powder
1 tsp salt
½ tsp chilli powder
1 large tomato, cut into rings, for garnish

1. Wash the rice and leave to soak in the water for about 1 hour.
2. Bring the water containing the rice to the boil, and then simmer gently for a further 15 minutes.
3. Transfer the contents to a colander to drain the rice.
4. Heat the oil in a big wok or a deep frying pan. Add the black mustard seeds, cumin and asafoetida, and cook them for a few seconds. Add the onion and cook until it is golden brown. Add the potato and cook over a low heat for about 10 minutes. Make sure that the potato is well cooked.
5. Add the rice, turmeric powder, salt and chilli powder and stir well. Cook the whole mixture together for a further 3 minutes stirring continuously.
6. Transfer the contents to a serving dish. Garnish with the fresh tomato and serve hot.

MATAR-BHAAT

This is a delicious alternative to plain boiled rice. The fluffy grains of rice dotted with peas in this recipe look very attractive. This is an ideal dish to serve at a dinner party. In order to keep the grains of rice whole be very gentle when stirring.

Cooking and preparation time: 27 minutes   *Serves:* 3–4

225g (8 oz) basmati rice
2 tbsp cooking oil
2 tbsp ghee (page 246)
1 tsp cumin seeds
1 tsp mustard seeds
115g (4 oz) frozen peas, defrosted
1 tsp salt
boiling water for cooking

1. Wash the rice in two or three changes of water and soak for 15 minutes.
2. In a large heavy based pan, heat the oil and the ghee together. When hot, add the cumin and mustard seeds. Allow to 'pop' for a few seconds with the lid on the pan, then add the peas. Cook for 2 minutes over medium heat.
3. Strain the rice and add to the pan with the salt and stir fry for 2 minutes.
4. Now add boiling water until it covers the rice completely and comes up to approximately 2.5cm (1 in) above the level of the rice. Cover the pan and cook until the liquid has been absorbed. This should take 5–7 minutes.
5. Test a grain of rice by pressing between the thumb and forefinger. If further cooking is required, sprinkle a little water into the pan and cook on a very low heat until tender.

SPICED RICE

This is a simple rice dish with just a hint of spice. It is good served with any of the saks.

Cooking and preparation time: 1 hour 15 minutes   *Serves:* 4

**250g (9 oz) basmati or long grain rice, washed and
    soaked for at least 30 minutes**
1 tbsp oil
4 cloves
4 black peppercorns
1 tsp cumin seeds
2.5cm (1 in) cinnamon stick
3 cardamom pods, opened
1 very small onion, sliced
250ml (½ pt) water
2 tsp salt

1. Wash and soak the rice. Drain.
2. Heat the oil and add all the spices and onion.
3. When the onion is soft, add the rice.
4. Add the water and salt, stir and bring to the boil.
5. Lower the heat, cover and simmer for 40 minutes until the rice is soft to touch.

Note: to prevent the rice from going mushy, do not stir during cooking.

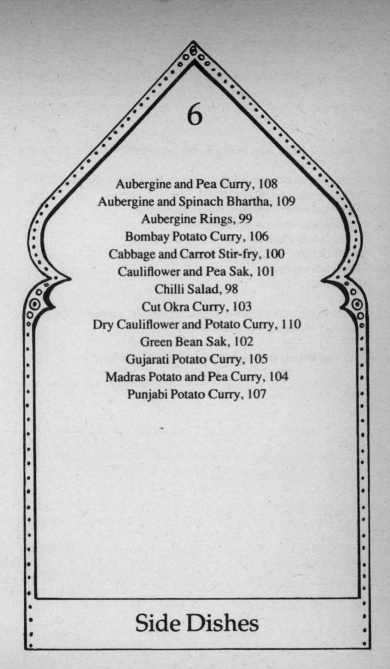

6

Side Dishes

CHILLI SALAD

This special salad, using fresh ingredients and dressed with a hint of malt vinegar, can be served with Peas and Potato Pilau or Meat Pilau (pages 86 and 117), or as an accompaniment with any main course.

Preparation time: 30 minutes + chilling time   *Serves:* 4

1 large carrot, quartered lengthways and finely sliced
1 large onion, very finely sliced
200g (7 oz) white cabbage, finely shredded
¼ cucumber, cut into small cubes
4 red or white radishes, cut into small cubes
3 green chillies, very finely chopped
4 tbsp malt vinegar
salt to taste

1. Mix all the ingredients together and leave covered in the fridge for at least 40 minutes before serving.

Note: wash hands thoroughly after handling chillies.

AUBERGINE RINGS

This can be served as a side dish at a dinner party. Prepared in advance it can then be kept warm in an oven or be re-heated in a microwave oven just before serving. The stacks of vegetables (layers of aubergines and potatoes) in this recipe should be kept intact during cooking.

Serve with freshly made chapattis or rice and Kadhi (page 56).

Cooking and preparation time: 15–22 minutes   *Serves:* 4–6

1 tsp salt
1 tsp ground turmeric
1½ tsp chilli powder
3 tbsp ground coriander
2 tbsp gram flour
2 tsp granulated sugar
8 tbsp cooking oil
1 large aubergine
water
1 large potato
3 tbsp natural yoghurt

1. In a small bowl put the salt, turmeric, chilli powder, ground coriander, gram flour, sugar and 3 tablespoons of the oil. Mix to a smooth paste.
2. Wash and slice the aubergine into thick rings and keep immersed in water to prevent discolouration of the flesh. Peel and slice the potato into thick rings.
3. Take the remainder of the oil in a large frying pan. Drain the aubergine and potato slices and spread out on a board. Rub the masala paste on one side of all the slices. Make up piles of vegetables in the frying pan with the masala side up, in alternate layers, starting with aubergine slices.
4. Cook, covered, over a very low heat until the vegetables are tender.
5. Spoon the yoghurt over all the vegetable piles and gently turn each pile over. Cook with the lid off for 2 minutes and serve.

CABBAGE AND CARROT STIR-FRY

This is a side dish that can be prepared in just a few minutes. Serve it instead of a salad when accompanied by a dish from the pulses section of this book. Alternatively, rolled up in a chapatti it makes a quick and easy lunch.

Cooking and preparation time: 7–8 minutes   *Serves:* 4–6

225g (8 oz) carrots
225g (8 oz) white cabbage
3 green chillies
6 tbsp cooking oil
2 tsp mustard seeds
¼ tsp asafoetida powder (optional)
1 tsp salt

1. Peel and grate the carrots thickly. Shred the cabbage finely. Split each one of the chillies lengthways into four (and wash hands thoroughly after handling them).
2. Heat the oil in a wok or a large frying pan. Add the mustard seeds, cover, and allow to 'pop' for a few seconds. Add the asafoetida and then immediately throw in the rest of the ingredients. Stir fry for a minute or two, according to preference. The vegetables should be crisp and crunchy.

CAULIFLOWER AND PEA SAK

This is a spicy vegetable dish that can be served as a side dish at a dinner party or for supper rolled up in freshly made chapattis with a squeeze of lemon. (The word 'sak' means it is a vegetable dish with little or no sauce.)

Cooking and preparation time: 12–20 minutes   *Serves:* 3–4

6 tbsp cooking oil
1 tsp mustard seeds
1 tsp cumin seeds
1 medium cauliflower, divided into florets
1½ tsp salt
1 tsp ground turmeric
225g (8 oz) frozen peas
1½ tsp chilli powder
2 tbsp ground coriander
½ tsp garam masala to serve

1. Heat the oil in a large heavy pan. Add the mustard and cumin seeds and cover the pan for a few seconds until the 'popping' stops.
2. Add the cauliflower, salt and turmeric and toss to cover the florets with oil.
3. Add the peas, chilli powder and ground coriander. Toss again to coat evenly.
4. Turn the heat down to low, cover tightly and cook until the cauliflower is tender.
5. Sprinkle with garam masala (page 247) and serve.

GREEN BEAN SAK

Any variety of green beans can be used for this dish but the best ones are the stringless varieties. Frozen green beans can also be used for this recipe but add 150ml (5 fl oz) of water with the salt, chilli powder, turmeric, etc. and cook very slowly until tender. Serve this dish with freshly made chapattis (page 71).

Cooking and preparation time: 20–25 minutes   *Serves:* 4–6

450g (1 lb) stringless green beans
1 large onion
3 tbsp cooking oil
1 tsp carom seeds (see Glossary)
1 tsp salt
1 tsp chilli powder
1 tsp ground turmeric
1 tbsp ground coriander
1 × 225g (8 oz) can tomatoes

1. Top and tail the beans and wash thoroughly. Slice thinly lengthways and cut into 5cm (2 in) pieces. Slice the onion.
2. Heat the oil, add the carom seeds and, after they have sizzled, add the prepared beans and onion. Add the salt, chilli powder, turmeric and ground coriander and mix well.
3. Reduce the heat and cook, covered, for 10 minutes or until the beans are tender. Chop the tomatoes, add to the beans and cook for another 5 minutes.

CUT OKRA CURRY

Okra, also sometimes called ladies' fingers, is a very popular vegetable in India. Like most vegetable curries, this is usually served with dhal and rice, or meat curry and rice. It may also be served with chapattis alone. For this recipe you need a liquidiser.

Cooking and preparation time: 45 minutes   *Serves:* 4

25g (1 oz) fresh garlic, peeled
2 green chillies
55g (2 oz) fresh ginger, peeled
340g (12 oz) fresh okra
90ml (3 fl oz) cooking oil
340g (12 oz) onions, chopped into large pieces
2 tsp tomato purée
1 tsp salt
½ tsp chilli powder
½ tsp turmeric powder
1 tsp garam masala
1 fresh tomato, cut into small pieces, for garnish

1. Place the garlic, green chillies, and ginger into a liquidiser and chop finely.
2. Wash the okra and then dry each piece individually with kitchen roll paper. This is very important as okra should be as dry as possible.
3. Cut the okra into 1cm (½ in) long pieces, lengthways.
4. Heat the oil to a high temperature, in a pan, add the contents of the liquidiser, and cook for a few seconds. Add the onions and cook together, stirring continuously, until the onions are very light brown. Add the tomato purée, salt, chilli powder, turmeric powder, and garam masala. Cook for a few seconds, and add the okra. Stir continuously for 2 to 3 minutes.
5. Reduce the heat, cover the pan and simmer gently for about 25 minutes. The heat must be kept very low, and the mixture needs to be stirred every 5–7 minutes.
6. Transfer the okra curry into a serving dish and garnish with the fresh tomato pieces.

MADRAS POTATO AND PEA CURRY

This is one of the many vegetable dishes served with another main dish and rice.

Cooking and preparation time: 30 minutes   *Serves:* 4

340g (12 oz) potatoes
60ml (2 fl oz) cooking oil
½ tsp cumin seeds
½ tsp black mustard seeds
2 large onions, finely chopped
170g (6 oz) frozen peas
½ tsp chilli powder
½ tsp turmeric powder
1 tsp madras curry powder
1 tsp salt
2 tsp tomato purée
300ml (½ pt) water
small amount green coriander, chopped

1. Peel the potatoes and cut them into about 2.5cm (1 in) cubes.
2. Heat the oil to a high temperature, in a large pan. Add the cumin, black mustard seeds and onions. Stir continuously and cook until the onions are golden brown. Add the potatoes, peas, chilli powder, turmeric powder, madras curry powder, salt and tomato purée. Stir continuously for 2 minutes. Add the water and bring to the boil. Lower the heat and simmer gently for about 20 minutes.
3. Transfer the curry to a serving dish and garnish with fresh green coriander.

GUJARATI POTATO CURRY

This is a very popular curry in a part of India which is well known for its vegetable dishes. It is usually served with some other curry (such as pulse or meat) and rice.

Cooking and preparation time: 35 minutes   *Serves:* 4

450g (1 lb) potatoes
30ml (1 fl oz) cooking oil
½ tsp cumin seeds
½ tsp black mustard seeds
¼ tsp asafoetida
½ tsp turmeric powder
½ tsp cumin powder
½ tsp coriander powder
1 tsp salt
1 tsp red chilli powder
55g (2 oz) canned tomatoes or
   2 tsp tomato purée
450ml (15 fl oz) water
small amount green coriander, chopped

1. Peel the potatoes and cut into about 2.5cm (1 in) cubes.
2. Heat the oil to a high temperature in a large pan and add the cumin and black mustard seeds and asafoetida. Leave to cook for a few seconds. Add the potatoes, turmeric powder, cumin powder, coriander powder, salt, chilli powder, and tomatoes (or purée). Stir continuously and cook for about 5 minutes.
3. Add the water and bring it to the boil. Lower the heat and simmer gently for about 20 minutes.
4. Place the curry in a serving dish and garnish with fresh coriander.

BOMBAY POTATO CURRY

This is a common curry in most Indian restaurants. It is very simple to cook and usually served with some other curry (such as pulse or meat) and rice.

Cooking and preparation time: 35 minutes   *Serves:* 4

450g (1 lb) potatoes
30ml (1 fl oz) cooking oil
1 tsp cumin seeds
½ tsp black mustard seeds
½ tsp turmeric powder
1 tsp salt
½ tsp chilli powder
4 oz fresh tomatoes, finely chopped
150ml (5 fl oz) water
small amount green coriander, chopped

1. Peel the potatoes and cut into 2.5cm (1 in) cubes.
2. Heat the oil to a high temperature in a large pan and add the cumin and black mustard seeds. Leave to cook for a few seconds. Add the potatoes, turmeric powder, salt, chilli powder and tomatoes. Stir continuously and cook for about 5 minutes.
3. Add the water and bring to the boil. Lower the heat and simmer gently for about 20 minutes.
4. Place the curry in a serving dish and garnish with fresh coriander.

PUNJABI POTATO CURRY

This is a popular curry in northern parts of India. It is usually served with parathas (page 78) or puris (deep fried chapattis – see recipe on page 74).

Cooking and preparation time: 35 minutes   *Serves:* 4

450g (1 lb) potatoes
25g (1 oz) butter
1 large onion, finely chopped
2 green chillies, finely chopped
1 tsp turmeric powder
1 tsp ginger powder
½ tsp coriander powder
1 tsp salt
½ tsp chilli powder
4 tsp tomato purée
240ml (8 fl oz) water
small amount green coriander, chopped

1. Wash the potatoes well.
2. Boil the potatoes, peel them and cut into 2.5cm (1 in) cubes.
3. Melt the butter in a large pan and add the onion and chillies. Stir and cook the onion and chillies until the onion is light brown. Now add the turmeric powder, ginger powder, coriander powder, salt, chilli powder, and tomato purée. Stir continuously and cook for about 2 minutes. Add half of the water, stir, and add the potatoes. Mix well and let it cook for about 3 minutes.
4. Add the remaining water and bring it to the boil. Lower the heat and simmer gently for about 5 minutes.
5. Place the curry in a serving dish and garnish with fresh coriander.

AUBERGINE AND PEA CURRY

This is a mild curry usually served with chapattis, parathas or a meat dish.

Cooking and preparation time: 25 minutes   *Serves:* 4

450g (1 lb) aubergines
600ml (1 pt) water for soaking
60ml (2 fl oz) cooking oil
½ tsp black mustard seeds
½ tsp cumin seeds
2 tsp tomato purée
1 tsp turmeric powder
1 tsp salt
1 tsp chilli powder
1 tsp garam masala
1 tsp garlic powder
115ml (4 fl oz) water
8 oz (225g) frozen peas
2 tsp lemon juice
small amount green coriander, chopped

1. Remove the stalks from the aubergines and slice them lengthways, like large chips. Soak the aubergines in the 600ml (1 pt) of water for about 5 minutes.
2. Heat the oil to a high temperature, in a heavy-based saucepan. Add the whole black mustard seeds and whole cumin seeds and let it cook for a few seconds.
3. Remove the aubergines from the water and add them to the pot. Now add the tomato purée, turmeric powder, salt, chilli powder, garam masala and garlic powder. Mix well and cook for about 2–3 minutes.
4. Add the 115ml (4 fl oz) of water, cover the pan, reduce the heat and let the aubergines simmer for about 10 minutes, stirring every 4–5 minutes.
5. Add the peas and the lemon juice. Simmer for a further 7 minutes, stirring every 3–4 minutes.
6. Transfer the contents to a serving dish, garnish with the fresh coriander and serve while hot.

AUBERGINE AND SPINACH BHARTHA

A bhartha is usually served with chapattis or as a side dish. This is a hot vegetable dish of mashed aubergine and spinach.

Cooking and preparation time: 1 hour 10 minutes   *Serves:* 4

450g (1 lb) aubergines
450g (1 lb) fresh spinach
60ml (2 fl oz) cooking oil
1 large onion, finely chopped
115g (4 oz) plum tomatoes, peeled and finely chopped
1 tsp salt
1 tsp turmeric powder
1 tsp chilli powder
1 tsp coriander powder
1 tsp cumin powder
1 tsp garlic powder

1. Prick the aubergines with a fork and then roast them under the grill for about 30 minutes, turning every 7–8 minutes. When the aubergines have been well roasted, remove the stalks, peel the aubergines and cut into very small pieces or mash them.
2. Wash the spinach, and chop finely.
3. Heat the oil to a high temperature, in a large pan. Add the onion and cook, stirring continuously, until the onion is golden brown. Add the mashed aubergine, spinach, tomatoes, salt, turmeric powder, chilli powder, coriander powder, cumin powder, and garlic powder. Stir and mix well. Lower the heat, cover the pan and let it simmer for about 25 minutes, stirring every 5–7 minutes.
4. Transfer the contents to a serving dish and serve while hot.

DRY CAULIFLOWER AND POTATO CURRY

This is a mild vegetable curry, especially good when served with a meat and pulse dish. It is also very popular with vegetarians. It is usually served with rice, chapattis or bread.

Cooking and preparation time: 35 minutes   *Serves:* 4

340g (12 oz) potatoes
340g (12 oz) cauliflower
60ml (2 fl oz) cooking oil
½ tsp cumin seeds
½ tsp black mustard seeds
1 tsp turmeric powder
1 tsp garam masala
2 tsp tomato purée
1 tsp salt
½ tsp chilli powder
120ml (4 fl oz) water
small amount green coriander, chopped

1. Peel the potatoes and cut them into 2.5cm (1 in) cubes.
2. Cut the cauliflower into small florets.
3. Heat the oil to a high temperature, in a pan. Add the cumin and black mustard seeds and leave to cook for a few seconds. Add the potatoes, cauliflower, turmeric powder, garam masala, tomato purée, salt and chilli powder. Stir continuously and cook for about 3 minutes.
4. Add the water, bring it to the boil and simmer gently for about 15 minutes.
5. Place the curry in a serving dish and garnish with fresh coriander.

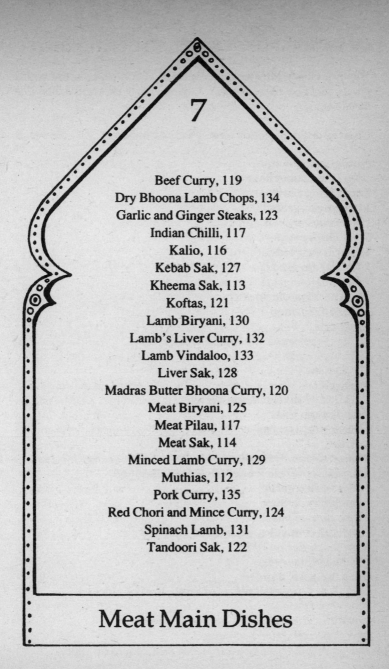

7

Beef Curry, 119
Dry Bhoona Lamb Chops, 134
Garlic and Ginger Steaks, 123
Indian Chilli, 117
Kalio, 116
Kebab Sak, 127
Kheema Sak, 113
Koftas, 121
Lamb Biryani, 130
Lamb's Liver Curry, 132
Lamb Vindaloo, 133
Liver Sak, 128
Madras Butter Bhoona Curry, 120
Meat Biryani, 125
Meat Pilau, 117
Meat Sak, 114
Minced Lamb Curry, 129
Muthias, 112
Pork Curry, 135
Red Chori and Mince Curry, 124
Spinach Lamb, 131
Tandoori Sak, 122

Meat Main Dishes

MUTHIAS

This is a type of stew made in heaven! Try this recipe and you'll never look back. Serve hot as a main meal with chapattis and rice or on its own.

Cooking and preparation time: 1 hour 40 minutes   *Serves:* 6

For the dumplings
150g (5 oz) millet flour
2 tsp garlic, crushed
2 tsp ginger, grated
1 level tsp salt
¼ tsp chilli powder
2 tbsp desiccated coconut
¼ tsp garam masala
1 handful fenugreek leaves, chopped
pinch of turmeric powder
juice of ½ a lemon
1 tbsp oil
125ml (¼ pt) water (and more if required)

For the stew
4 tbsp oil
2 × 2.5cm (1 in) cinnamon sticks
3 cardamom pods
7 black peppercorns
6 cloves
2 large onions, finely sliced
3 handfuls of fresh fenugreek leaves, chopped
4 tsp crushed garlic
4 tsp ginger, grated
2 tbsp tomato purée
450g (1 lb) tomatoes, peeled and chopped
3 tsp coriander powder
1–2 tsp chilli powder
½ tsp turmeric powder
510g (1 lb 2 oz) small pieces of lamb, beef or chicken
200g (7 oz) peas
1 medium aubergine, cut into small pieces
1 large bunch spinach, chopped
2 saragvo singh (see Glossary), cut into 7cm (3 in) pieces

3 handfuls of fresh coriander leaves, chopped
200g (7 oz) Indian beans, halved
150g (5 oz) coconut cream
salt to taste
375ml (¾ pt) water
4 medium sized potatoes, peeled and cut into halves

1. Mix together the dumpling ingredients and bind into a dough with the oil and water. Shape into small sausage type dumplings.
2. *For the stew:* heat the oil, add the whole spices and fry with the onions until golden brown.
3. Add the fenugreek leaves, garlic and ginger.
4. Add the tomato purée and allow to cook for at least 1 minute.
5. Then add all the other ingredients *except* for the potatoes and dumplings.
6. When the vegetables are half cooked (about 20 minutes), add the potatoes and dumplings.
7. Allow to boil and then turn the heat to low, cover and simmer for 1 hour.
8. Stir occasionally, and add extra water if necessary.

KHEEMA SAK

Very easy to make, this is a mouth-watering minced meat dish. Serve as a main course with chapattis and rice.

Cooking and preparation time: 50 minutes   *Serves:* 4–6

3 tbsp oil
1 large onion, sliced
4 cloves
4 cardamom pods, opened
6 black peppercorns
2.5cm (1 in) cinnamon stick
2 tsp garlic, crushed
2 tsp ginger, grated
1 tbsp tomato purée

(continued overleaf)

150g (5 oz) tomatoes, peeled and chopped
½ tsp turmeric powder
½ tsp chilli powder
2 tsp coriander powder
3 medium sized potatoes, peeled and quartered
450g (1 lb) mince
125–250ml (¼–½ pt) water
salt to taste
handful of fresh coriander leaves, chopped, for garnish

1. Heat the oil and add the onion and whole spices.
2. When the onion has browned, add the garlic and ginger and fry for 3 minutes.
3. Then add the tomato purée and let it stand in the oil for at least 2 minutes before stirring.
4. Now add the rest of the ingredients (*except* the coriander leaves), cover and simmer for 30 minutes, until the potatoes and mince have cooked.
5. Garnish with chopped coriander leaves before serving.

MEAT SAK

The combination of spices makes this a very simple but effective dish. Serve as a main course with chapattis, rice and a salad.

Cooking and preparation time: 1 hour   *Serves:* 4–6

5 tbsp oil
8 cloves
8 black peppercorns
4 cardamom pods
2.5cm (1 in) cinnamon stick
1 large onion, sliced
2 tsp ginger, grated
2 tsp garlic, crushed
2 tbsp tomato purée

250g (9 oz) tomatoes, peeled and chopped
4 tsp coriander powder
¼ tsp turmeric powder
½ tsp chilli powder
1 tsp garam masala
2 whole green chillies, split in half lengthwise (optional)
salt to taste
800g (1 lb 12 oz) lamb or beef cubes
2 medium sized potatoes, cut into quarters
125ml (¼ pt) water or stock*
chopped coriander leaves to garnish

1. Heat the oil, add the whole spices and onion.
2. When the onion is golden brown, add the ginger and garlic and fry for 2 minutes.
3. Then add the tomato purée and fry for a further minute.
4. Add the tomatoes, powders, garam masala, chillies (if using) and salt. Stir.
5. Add the meat and potatoes. Stir.
6. Add 125ml (¼ pt) water, cover and simmer on low heat for 40 minutes until the meat is cooked. Keep checking to ensure the sauce is not drying up before the meat is cooked, and add more water if necessary.
7. Garnish with the chopped coriander.

Note: always wash hands thoroughly after handling chillies.

* The meat could be pre-cooked with a handful of chopped onion mixed with crushed garlic/ginger, a few cloves and peppercorns, cardamom, a small stick of cinnamon, 2 tsp of whole cumin seeds and 240ml (8 fl oz) water. The stock is then used to make the sauce instead of just water.

KALIO

An excellent combination of flavours makes this a rich dish! Serve as a main course, with chapattis or naan bread and Spiced Rice (page 96).

Cooking and preparation time: 1 hour 40 minutes   *Serves:* 4–6

oil for deep frying
2 large onions, sliced
4 medium sized potatoes, quartered
800g (1 lb 12 oz) beef cubes
3 tsp garlic, crushed
3 tsp ginger, grated
4 green chillies, finely sliced
250g (9 oz) tomatoes, peeled and chopped
2 tbsp tomato purée
1 tsp garam masala
½ tsp turmeric powder
½ tsp chilli powder
3 tsp coriander powder
150g (5 fl oz) plain yoghurt
pinch of saffron
6 cloves
6 black peppercorns
4 cardamom pods, opened
2.5cm (1 in) cinnamon stick
handful of coriander leaves, chopped
salt to taste

1. Deep fry the onions and potatoes until golden brown (the potatoes do not need to be fully cooked at this stage).
2. Remove the onions and potatoes and set the oil aside. (You can use it to make a sak.)
3. Put all the ingredients into a large saucepan (including the onions and potatoes), mix, cover and allow to simmer on a low heat for 1 hour, until the beef is tender.

Note: wash hands thoroughly after handling chillies.

INDIAN CHILLI

This is a hot dish made with minced meat and kidney beans. Serve with rice and plain yoghurt.

Cooking and preparation time: 1 hour   *Serves:* 4

3 tbsp oil
1 large onion, chopped
450g (1 lb) minced beef
2 tsp garlic, crushed
2 tsp ginger, grated
400g (14 oz) tomatoes, peeled and chopped
1 tbsp tomato purée
1 tbsp coriander powder
1 tsp chilli powder
2 whole chillies
1 capsicum pepper, chopped
400g (14 oz) kidney beans (see page 13)
250ml (½ pt) water
salt to taste

1. Heat the oil in a saucepan and fry the onion until very lightly brown.
2. Add the minced beef, garlic and ginger and fry until the beef turns brown.
3. Add the rest of the ingredients, bring to the boil, cover and simmer for 50 minutes.

MEAT PILAU

Savoury rice, great as a main course with Chilli Salad (page 98), raita and pickles.

Cooking and preparation time: 2 hours   *Serves:* 4–6

(continued overleaf)

450g (1 lb) rice, washed and soaked for 40 minutes
510g (1 lb 2 oz) lamb, beef or chicken pieces
250ml (½ pt) water
4 tsp garlic, crushed
4 tsp ginger, grated
4 green chillies, whole or chopped
3 tbsp oil
1 large onion, sliced
2 tsp cumin seeds
3 cardamom pods
2 × 2.5cm (1 in) sticks cinnamon
8 cloves
8 black peppercorns
handful of coriander leaves, chopped
150g (5 oz) tomatoes, peeled and chopped
6 small potatoes, peeled and cut into halves
250ml (½ pt) stock* or water
salt to taste
25g (1 oz) butter or margarine

1. Wash and soak the rice, then drain it.
2. Put the meat or chicken in a saucepan with the measured quantity of water, add half of the garlic, ginger and chillies and cook for 30 minutes, until tender.
3. Heat the oil in a separate saucepan.
4. Add the onion, cumin seeds, cardamom pods, cinnamon, cloves and peppercorns.
5. When the onion has softened, add the remaining garlic, ginger and chillies and cook for 2 minutes.
6. Next, add the meat or chicken, the coriander, tomatoes, rice and potatoes.
7. If the meat has been pre-cooked (see below*) add the resulting stock, made up to 250ml (½ pt) with more water if required. If the meat has not been pre-cooked, just add the same quantity of water.

* The meat could be pre-cooked with a handful of chopped onions mixed with crushed garlic/ginger, a few cloves and peppercorns, cardamom, a small stick of cinnamon, 2 tsp of cumin seeds and 250ml (½ pt) water. The stock is then used to make the sauce instead of just water.

8. Add salt to taste, bring to the boil, cover and simmer on low heat for 40 minutes, until the rice has cooked.
9. Add the butter or margarine in blobs while the pilau is hot.

Note: always wash hands thoroughly after handling chillies.
To prevent rice going mushy, never stir while it is cooking.

BEEF CURRY

This is a hot curry. It can be eaten on its own, but is usually served with boiled noodles, rice, chapattis, bread, puris, parathas, mashed potatoes, or pitta bread. For this recipe you need a liquidiser.

Cooking and preparation time: 1 hour 40 minutes   *Serves:* 4

450g (1 lb) shin or stewing beef
10g (½ oz) fresh garlic, peeled
10g (½ oz) fresh ginger, peeled
2 green chillies
55g (2 oz) plum tomatoes, peeled
30ml (1 fl oz) cooking oil
1 large onion, finely chopped
½ tsp turmeric powder
1 tsp tomato purée
½ tsp chilli powder
1 tsp garam masala
1 tsp salt
1 tsp tandoori masala
4 tsp soy sauce
600ml (1 pt) water
small amount green coriander, chopped

1. Cut the beef into about 2.5cm (1 in) cubes.
2. Place the garlic, ginger, green chillies, and tomatoes into a liquidiser, and blend them into a thick paste.
3. Heat the oil in a pan to a high temperature. Add the chopped

(continued overleaf)

119

onion and cook until it is golden brown. Add the beef cubes, blended paste, turmeric powder, tomato purée, chilli powder, garam masala, salt, tandoori masala, and soy sauce. Stir continuously for about 2 minutes. Reduce the heat, cover the pan and let it cook for about 20 minutes, stirring every few minutes. Add the water and stir. Simmer gently for a further hour.

4. Transfer the curry into a serving dish, and garnish with the fresh coriander.

MADRAS BUTTER BHOONA CURRY

This is a medium dry beef curry, usually served with rice or chapattis.

Cooking and preparation time: 1 hour 20 minutes   *Serves:* 4

450g (1 lb) stewing beef
25g (1 oz) butter
1 large onion, finely chopped
55g (2 oz) plum tomatoes, peeled and finely chopped
1 tsp tomato purée
1 tsp salt
1 tsp turmeric powder
1 tsp chilli powder
2 tsp madras curry powder
1 tsp garlic powder
450ml (15 fl oz) water
small amount green coriander, chopped

1. Cut the beef into 2.5cm (1 in) cubes.
2. Melt the butter in a large pan; add the onion and cook until golden brown, stirring continuously.
3. Add the tomatoes, tomato purée, salt, turmeric powder, chilli powder, madras curry powder, garlic powder and the cubes of beef, and mix well. Stir continuously and cook for about 5 minutes.

4. Add the water, reduce the heat and simmer for about 1 hour stirring every 8 to 10 minutes.

5. Transfer the contents to a serving dish and garnish with the coriander.

KOFTAS

These beef meatballs are particularly good if you like mince dishes. They can be served with rice or chapattis. They can also be served with English side dishes such as boiled potatoes, cabbage or cauliflower. For this recipe you need a liquidiser.

Cooking and preparation time: 1 hour 50 minutes   *Serves:* 4

25g (1 oz) fresh garlic, peeled
25g (1 oz) fresh ginger, peeled
3 green chillies
450g (1 lb) minced beef
1 tsp salt
½ tsp chilli powder
2 tsp tandoori masala
1 tsp garam masala
2 tsp tomato purée
small amount green coriander, chopped
30ml (1 fl oz) cooking oil
2 medium sized onions, finely chopped
55g (2 oz) plum tomatoes, peeled
300ml (½ pt) water

1. Place the garlic, ginger and green chillies into a liquidiser and process until finely chopped.

2. Mix the contents of the liquidiser with the mince, salt, chilli powder, tandoori masala, garam masala, tomato purée and fresh coriander and mix well. Shape the mixture into small meatballs approximately 5cm (2 in) in diameter, and place them on a tray. Cover the tray.

(continued overleaf)

3. Heat the oil in a large cooking pan. Add the onions and fry until they are golden brown. Now add the tomatoes and cook for a further 2 minutes.

4. Gently place six to eight meatballs in the pan. Cover the pan, lower the heat and simmer for about 20 minutes. The meatballs will shrink in size and become golden brown. Carefully remove these balls from the onion and tomato mixture and place them on one side. Add another six to eight fresh mince balls to the onion and tomato mixture, cover and simmer again for about the same period. Repeat this process until all the meatballs are done.

5. Now add all the meatballs to the onion and tomato mixture. Stir very gently and simmer for a further 50 minutes. Add the water, bring it to the boil, and simmer for a further 45 minutes, stirring every 10 minutes.

6. Transfer the contents to a serving dish and serve while hot.

TANDOORI SAK

A rich tandoori-flavoured curry eaten as the main course. Serve with Naan Bread (page 70) and Spiced Rice (page 96).

Cooking and preparation time: 3 hours   *Serves:* 4–6

800g (1 lb 12 oz) beef
150g (5 oz) carton of plain yoghurt
4 tsp garlic, crushed
4 tsp ginger, grated
5 tbsp tandoori powder
1 tsp chilli powder
1 tbsp oil
250g (9 oz) tomatoes, peeled and chopped
1 tbsp tomato purée
2 tsp coriander powder
salt to taste
oil for frying
1 large onion, sliced

1. Marinade the beef in a mixture of all of the above ingredients, *except* for the oil and onion, for at least 2 hours, preferably overnight.
2. Heat the oil and fry the onion until dark brown, looking as though it were almost burnt and add to the marinade mixture in a large saucepan.
3. Cover and simmer for 1 hour, until the meat is tender.

GARLIC AND GINGER STEAKS

These are luxurious and a delicious way of cooking steaks. Serve hot with fried, chipped potatoes and tamarind.

Cooking and preparation time: 1 hour   *Serves:* 6
                                     + marinating overnight (optional)

4 tsp garlic, crushed
3 tsp ginger, grated
3 crushed chillies
2 tsp garam masala
2 tsp salt
1 tsp ground black pepper
2 tbsp oil
6 × 170g (6 oz) steaks

1. Mix together the garlic, ginger, chillies, garam masala, salt, ground black pepper and the oil.
2. Cut fine slits in the steaks and rub the above mixture into them, on both sides.
3. Heat a grill on high and cook the steaks until they brown on both sides.

Note: these taste even better if they are marinaded in the above mixture overnight.
Wash hands thoroughly after handling chillies.

RED CHORI AND MINCE CURRY

If you do not like beans but would like to try something similar to chilli con carne, then mince with red lentil-type seeds is the dish for you. This mince curry is usually served with rice or chapattis. It can also be served with chips. For this recipe you need a liquidiser.

Note: the chori must be boiled for about 45 minutes as indicated in the recipe otherwise it could cause indigestion.

Cooking and preparation time: 10 hours 30 minutes   *Serves:* 4

55g (2 oz) red chori
450ml (15 fl oz) water for boiling red chori
10g (½ oz) fresh garlic, peeled
25g (1 oz) fresh ginger, peeled
2 green chillies
30ml (1 fl oz) cooking oil
1 large onion, finely chopped
1 tsp tomato purée
½ tsp turmeric powder
½ tsp chilli powder
½ tsp tandoori masala
1 tsp garam masala
½ tsp salt
4 tsp soy sauce
225g (8 oz) minced beef
300ml (½ pt) water for cooking
small amount green coriander, chopped

1. Wash the red chori, like all pulses, and leave to soak in about 600ml (1 pt) of cold water for about 8 hours. (See page 12 on how to wash pulses.)
2. Strain the chori and put in a pan. Add the 450ml (15 fl oz) of water. Place the pan on a hot ring, and bring the water to the boil. When the water has started to boil, cover the pan, lower the heat and simmer for a further 45 minutes.
3. Place the garlic, ginger and green chillies into a liquidiser and chop very finely.
4. Heat the cooking oil in a large pan to a high temperature. Add the onion and cook until it is golden brown.
5. Add the contents of the liquidiser, tomato purée, turmeric powder,

chilli powder, tandoori masala, garam masala, salt and soy sauce. Cook this mixture for about 2 minutes.

6. Now add the boiled chori and the mince. Simmer gently for another 15 minutes stirring every 5 minutes.

7. Add the 300ml (½ pt) of water, cover the pan and let it simmer for a further 45 minutes. Stir every 5 minutes.

8. Transfer the curry into a serving dish and garnish with fresh coriander. Serve while hot.

MEAT BIRYANI

This is an absolutely delicious dish of beef in a rich sauce between layers of rice. It's easy to make, too! Serve as a main course, with plain yoghurt and pickles of your choice.

Cooking and preparation time: 2 hours 40 minutes   *Serves:* 4–6

675g (1½ lb) rice, washed and soaked for 40 minutes

For the sauce
oil for deep frying
2 large onions, sliced
4 medium sized potatoes, quartered
675g (1½ lb) beef, cubed
3 tsp garlic, crushed
3 tsp ginger, grated
4 green chillies, finely sliced
250g (9 oz) tomatoes, peeled and chopped
2 tbsp tomato purée
1 tsp garam masala
½ tsp turmeric powder
½ tsp chilli powder
3 tsp coriander powder
150g (5 oz) carton plain yoghurt
pinch of saffron
6 cloves
6 black peppercorns
4 cardamom pods, opened

(continued overleaf)

2.5cm (1 in) cinnamon stick
handful of coriander leaves, chopped
3 hard boiled eggs (optional)
salt to taste

For the rice
1 litre (2 pts) or more of water, to cook the rice
1 tbsp salt (or to taste)

For the topping
2 tbsp oil
4 cloves
4 black peppercorns
4 cardamom pods, opened
2.5cm (1 in) cinnamon stick
1 tsp whole cumin seeds
1 tbsp yellow food colouring

1. *To make the sauce:* deep fry the onions and potatoes, separately, until golden brown (the potatoes do not need to be fully cooked at this stage). Set the oil aside.
2. Mix all the ingredients (*except* a handful of onions, to be used later) in a large saucepan, cover and simmer on a low heat for 1 hour, until the beef is tender.
3. *For the rice:* boil the washed, soaked and drained rice for 25 minutes until just cooked (i.e. not mushy) and drain.
4. Take a big ovenproof dish and make alternate layers with the sauce, the rice, the sauce and finally the rice as the top layer.
5. *For the topping:* heat the oil and add all the ingredients *except* for the food colouring.
6. When the cumin seeds start to fry, remove from the heat and spread over the top layer of rice.
7. Sprinkle the top with the remaining fried onions (saved from earlier) and pour the yellow food colouring over the rice in the shape of a cross.
8. Cover and place in a pre-heated oven at 160°C (325°F), gas mark 3 for 50 minutes, until the biryani has heated through.

Note: to prevent rice from going mushy, never stir while it is cooking.
Wash hands thoroughly after handling chillies.
The layers should be kept distinct when serving up this dish.

KEBAB SAK

This is a type of meatball curry, made with fried kebabs in a delicious sauce. Serve as a main course with chapattis and rice.

Cooking and preparation time: 2 hours   *Serves:* 4-6

Refer to page 61 for the recipe for kebabs

For the sauce
2 tbsp oil
5 cloves
5 black peppercorns
3 cardamom pods, opened
2.5cm (1 in) cinnamon stick
1 large onion, sliced
3 tsp garlic, crushed
2 tsp ginger, grated
1 tbsp tomato purée
150g (5 oz) tomatoes, peeled and chopped
125ml (¼ pt) water (and more if required)
salt to taste
handful chopped coriander leaves for garnish

1. Follow the recipe on page 61 and make the kebabs.
2. *For the sauce:* heat the oil and add the whole spices and onion.
3. When the onion has turned golden brown, add the garlic, ginger and tomato purée and fry for 2-3 minutes.
4. Then add the rest of the ingredients (*except* the coriander and the kebabs), stir and cook for 5 minutes.
5. Finally, add about 15 kebabs (do not stir), cover and simmer for 30 minutes.
6. Garnish with chopped coriander leaves before serving.

LIVER SAK

An unusual combination of flavours makes this dish distinct. Serve as a main course with Spiced Rice (page 96) or for breakfast with fried eggs and parathas.

Cooking and preparation time: 1 hour   *Serves:* 4–6

3 tbsp oil
5 cloves
5 black peppercorns
3 cardamom pods, opened
2.5cm (1 in) cinnamon stick
1 large onion, sliced
250g (9 oz) liver, cut into small pieces
3 tsp garlic, crushed
1 tsp ginger, grated
1 tbsp tomato purée
150g (5 oz) tomatoes, peeled and chopped
¼ tsp turmeric powder
½ tsp chilli powder
3 tsp coriander powder
3 medium sized potatoes, peeled and quartered
125ml (¼ pt) water (and more if required)
salt to taste
handful of chopped coriander leaves for garnish

1. Heat the oil, add the whole spices and onion and fry until the onion is golden brown.
2. Add the liver and fry until brown.
3. Add the garlic and ginger, fry for 1 minute and then add the tomato purée and fry for a further minute.
4. Then add the rest of the ingredients (*except* the chopped coriander), stir, cover and simmer for 40 minutes, until the liver and potatoes have cooked. (While cooking, keep checking to see if more water is required.)
5. Garnish with the chopped coriander leaves before serving.

MINCED LAMB CURRY

This is a dry curry usually served with chapattis or pitta bread. It also makes an excellent filling for toasted sandwiches. Bay leaves may be added to give the curry a nice fragrance and a slightly sharper taste. For this recipe you need a liquidiser.

Cooking and preparation time: 50 minutes   *Serves:* 4

10g (½ oz) fresh garlic, peeled
25g (1 oz) fresh ginger, peeled
3 green chillies
60ml (2 fl oz) cooking oil
1 large onion, finely chopped
2 tsp tomato purée
1 tsp turmeric powder
1 tsp chilli powder
2 tsp tandoori masala
1 tsp garam masala
1 tsp salt
2 bay leaves (optional)
340g (12 oz) minced lamb
600ml (1 pt) water
small amount green coriander, chopped

1. Place the garlic, ginger, and green chillies into a liquidiser and chop finely.
2. Heat the oil in a pan and add the chopped onion. Cook the onion until it is golden brown. Now add the liquidiser contents, tomato purée, turmeric powder, chilli powder, tandoori masala, garam masala, salt (and bay leaves if used). Cook for a further 5 minutes, stirring continuously.
3. Add the mince, and cook for a further 5 minutes, stirring continuously.
4. Add the water, cover the pan, reduce the heat and simmer gently for a further 30 minutes, stirring every 5 to 7 minutes.
5. Transfer the contents to a serving dish and garnish with fresh green coriander. Serve while hot.
6. The bay leaves (if used) are discarded while eating and left on the plate.

LAMB BIRYANI

This is a mild rice dish, usually served with dhal or a vegetable dish.

Cooking and preparation time: 1 hour   *Serves:* 4

170g (6 oz) basmati rice
750ml (25 fl oz) water
1 small onion, finely chopped
1 green chilli, finely chopped
225g (8 oz) boneless lamb, cut into very small 1cm (½ in) cubes
½ tsp turmeric powder
1 tsp salt
½ tsp chilli powder
2 tsp soy sauce
85g (3 oz) frozen peas
85g (3 oz) frozen diced carrots

1. Wash the rice like all pulses, as described in the introduction.
2. In a large pan mix the water, onion, green chilli, lamb, turmeric powder, salt, chilli powder, and soy sauce. Bring to the boil, cover the pan, reduce the heat and let the mixture boil for about 35 minutes.
3. Add the washed rice, peas and carrots. Bring back to the boil and then reduce the heat again. Cover the pan and simmer gently for about 12 minutes. The rice should look dry.
4. Transfer the contents to a serving dish and serve hot.

SPINACH LAMB

Spinach is frequently used in Indian dishes, and spinach and lamb do make an excellent combination. This dish is quite mild, and can be served with chapattis, pitta bread, parathas or even bread. For this recipe you need a meat cleaver, or get your butcher to chop a leg of lamb up for you.

Cooking and preparation time: 1 hour 10 minutes   *Serves:* 4

675g (1½ lb) leg of lamb
340g (12 oz) spinach
60ml (2 fl oz) cooking oil
1 large onion, finely chopped
3 tsp tomato purée
1 tsp salt
1 tsp turmeric powder
½ tsp chilli powder
1 tsp garam masala
120ml (4 fl oz) water

1. Chop the leg of lamb into small pieces, about 2.5cm (1 in) in length. There is no need to remove the bones.
2. Cut the spinach into small pieces and wash well.
3. Heat the oil to a high temperature in a large pan. Add the onion and cook until the onion is golden brown. Add the tomato purée, salt, turmeric powder, chilli powder and garam masala. Stir well and let the mixture cook for about 1 minute.
4. Add the lamb, spinach and the water. Mix well, lower the heat and simmer gently for about 40 minutes, stirring every 5–7 minutes.
5. Transfer the contents to a serving dish and serve hot.
6. While eating, the bones are discarded and left on the plate.

LAMB'S LIVER CURRY

This liver curry is usually eaten on its own, or served with chapattis or bread but is not served with rice. It is normally very mild but green fresh chillies can be added to make it slightly hot. For this recipe you need a liquidiser.

Cooking and preparation time: 1 hour 10 minutes   *Serves:* 4

10g (½ oz) fresh garlic, peeled
25g (1 oz) fresh ginger, peeled
3 green chillies (optional for hot curry)
55g (2 oz) canned tomatoes
30ml (1 fl oz) cooking oil
1 large onion, finely chopped
450g (1 lb) lamb's liver, cut into small pieces
½ tsp turmeric powder
1 tsp tomato purée
½ tsp chilli powder
1 tsp tandoori masala
1 tsp salt
½ tsp garam masala
300ml (½ pt) water
small amount green coriander, chopped

1. Preheat the oven to 190°C (375°F), gas mark 5. Place the garlic, ginger, green chillies (if used), and tomatoes in a liquidiser and blend them into a thick paste.
2. Place the oil in a pan. When hot, add the chopped onion. Cook the onion until it is golden brown. Add the contents of the liquidiser, liver pieces, turmeric powder, tomato purée, chilli powder, tandoori masala, salt and garam masala. Cook for about 10 minutes, stirring constantly. Place the curry in a casserole. Add water and stir.
3. Cover the casserole, and cook on the middle shelf of the preheated oven for about 45–50 minutes.
4. Garnish with green coriander and serve while hot.

LAMB VINDALOO

This lamb and potato curry is a very hot curry usually served with rice, chapattis or parathas.

Cooking and preparation time: 1 hour   *Serves:* 4

450g (1 lb) potatoes
60ml (2 fl oz) cooking oil
1 large onion, finely chopped
6 green chillies, finely chopped
3 tsp tomato purée
2 tsp turmeric powder
2 tsp chilli powder
1 tsp garlic powder
1 tsp ginger powder
2 tsp salt
2 tsp garam masala
450g (1 lb) diced lamb
450g (15 fl oz) water
small amount green coriander, chopped

1. Peel the potatoes and cut into medium-large cubes (about 2.5cm (1 in) square).
2. Heat the oil to a high temperature in a large pan. Add the onion and chillies, and cook, stirring continuously, until the onion is golden brown.
3. Add the tomato purée, turmeric powder, chilli powder, garlic powder, ginger powder, salt, garam masala and the diced lamb. Mix well, lower the heat and simmer gently for about 5 minutes, stirring every 2–3 minutes.
4. Add the water and let the lamb simmer for about 35 minutes, stirring every 5–7 minutes.
5. Add the potatoes and simmer for another 20 minutes, stirring every 5–7 minutes.
6. Transfer the contents to a serving dish and garnish with green coriander.

DRY BHOONA LAMB CHOPS

This is a very dry and mild curry which can be served with fried rice, or even mashed potatoes or chips. For this recipe you need a wok or deep frying pan.

Cooking and preparation time: 1 hour   *Serves:* 4

8 lamb chops
90ml (3 fl oz) cooking oil
½ tsp cumin seeds
½ tsp black mustard seeds
225g (8 oz) onions, finely chopped
2 green chillies, finely chopped
115g (4 oz) canned tomatoes, finely chopped
1½ tsp salt
1 tsp turmeric powder
1½ tsp garam masala
½ tsp chilli powder
120ml (4 fl oz) water
small amount green coriander, chopped

1. Cut the fat from the lamb chops.
2. In a wok, or deep frying pan, heat the oil to a high temperature. Add the cumin and black mustard seeds and let it cook for a few seconds. Add the chopped onions and the green chillies. Stir continuously and cook until the onions are golden brown. Add the tomatoes and cook for about a minute. Add the salt, turmeric powder, garam masala and chilli powder. Cook this spicy mixture for about another minute.
3. Add the lamb chops. Mix well, cover the pan, lower the heat and let it simmer for about 10 minutes, stirring every 3–4 minutes.
4. Add the water, mix well and simmer for another 40 minutes stirring every 8–10 minutes.
5. Transfer the contents to a serving dish and garnish with the green coriander.

PORK CURRY

This is a dry hot curry. It can be eaten as a snack on its own, or served with mashed potatoes, chapattis, pitta bread or parathas. For this recipe you need a liquidiser.

Cooking and preparation time: 1 hour 10 minutes   *Serves:* 4

900g (2 lb) boneless pork
10g (½ oz) fresh garlic, peeled
10g (½ oz) fresh ginger, peeled
2 green chillies
225g (8 oz) fresh tomatoes
30ml (1 fl oz) cooking oil
1 large onion, finely chopped
½ tsp turmeric powder
½ tsp chilli powder
½ tsp tandoori masala
1 tsp salt
1 tsp garam masala
120ml (4 fl oz) water
small amount green coriander, chopped

1. Cut the pork pieces into about 2.5cm (1 in) cubes.
2. Blend the garlic, ginger and green chillies in a liquidiser until finely chopped.
3. Cut the tomatoes into small pieces.
4. Heat the oil in a pan to a high temperature; add the chopped onion and cook until it is golden brown.
5. Add the contents of the liquidiser, tomatoes, pork cubes, turmeric powder, chilli powder, tandoori masala, salt and garam masala. Stir continuously for about 2 minutes.
6. Reduce the heat, cover the pan and simmer gently for about 20 minutes, stirring every 5–7 minutes.
7. Add the water, stir and simmer gently for a further 30 minutes, again stirring every 5–7 minutes.
8. Transfer the curry to a serving dish. Garnish with fresh green coriander and serve while hot.

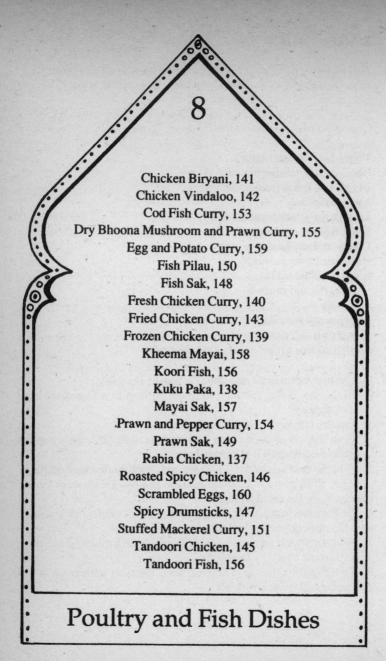

8

Poultry and Fish Dishes

RABIA CHICKEN

A dry, spicy chicken dish which can also be served as a starter with raita and salad or as an accompaniment to a main course.

Cooking and preparation time: 1 hour   *Serves:* 4

2 tbsp oil
3 tsp garlic, crushed
3 tsp ginger, grated
4 tbsp tomato purée
2 tsp coriander powder
1 tsp chilli powder (or to taste)
¼ tsp turmeric powder
1 tbsp tikka powder
1 tsp salt
8 chicken legs or thighs

1. Heat the oil and add the garlic, ginger and tomato purée and fry for 4 minutes.
2. Add the rest of the ingredients and stir frequently for 10 minutes over a medium heat.
3. Transfer to a baking tray and cook in the oven at 200°C (400°F), gas mark 6, for 40 minutes until the chicken is tender.

KUKU PAKA

A spiced chicken and coconut dish, full of exotic flavours! Serve with chapattis and rice.

Cooking and preparation time: 1 hour   *Serves:* 4–6

800g (1 lb 12 oz) chicken pieces
5 green chillies, finely chopped
2 whole chillies
4 tsp garlic, crushed
4 tsp ginger, grated
250g (9 oz) tomatoes, peeled and chopped
½ tsp turmeric powder
3 tbsp lemon juice
150g (5 oz) coconut cream
salt to taste
4 medium sized potatoes, cut into quarters
500ml (1 pt) water
1 large onion, sliced
4 hard boiled eggs (optional)
handful of chopped coriander leaves, for garnish

1. Put all the ingredients *except* the eggs and coriander into a big saucepan.
2. Bring to the boil, lower the heat, cover and simmer for at least 50 minutes, until the chicken is cooked.
3. Add the eggs and garnish with chopped coriander leaves.

Note: wash hands thoroughly after handling chillies. This dish can be re-heated, but do so gently.

FROZEN CHICKEN CURRY

This is a mild to medium hot chicken curry. It is usually served with a rice dish, or chapattis. You can either use fresh green chillies (if you like curry dishes hot) or a fresh green pepper for milder taste. Parsley or coriander can be used for garnishing. For this recipe you need a liquidiser.

Cooking and preparation time: 1 hour 20 minutes　　　*Serves:* 4

900g (2 lb) frozen chicken pieces (thawed)
25g (1 oz) fresh garlic, peeled
25g (1 oz) fresh ginger, peeled
3 green chillies or 1 green pepper (depending on taste)
60ml (2 fl oz) cooking oil
3 large onions, finely chopped
1 tsp turmeric powder
1 tsp chilli powder
2 tsp garam masala
1 tsp tandoori masala
3 tsp tomato purée
170g (6 oz) plum tomatoes, peeled
2 tsp salt
parsley or fresh green coriander

1. Remove the skin from the chicken pieces.
2. Place the garlic, ginger and green chillies (or green pepper) in a liquidiser and process until finely chopped.
3. Heat the oil to a high temperature in a pan. Add the chopped onions and cook until they are golden brown. Add the chicken pieces, the contents of the liquidiser, turmeric powder, chilli powder, garam masala, tandoori masala, tomato purée, tomatoes and salt. Stir continuously for a few minutes.
4. Reduce the heat and simmer for about 1 hour, stirring every 5–7 minutes, keeping the pan covered all the time.
5. Garnish with chopped parsley or fresh coriander.
6. The bones are discarded while eating and left on the plate.

FRESH CHICKEN CURRY

This is a very popular curry, usually served with rice or chapattis. It takes longer to cook than the frozen chicken curry, and tastes quite different.

Cooking and preparation time: 1 hour 50 minutes   *Serves:* 4

60ml (2 fl oz) cooking oil
2 large onions, finely chopped
900g (2 lb) fresh chicken, skinned and cut into small pieces
225g (8 oz) plum tomatoes, peeled
1 tsp salt
1 tsp chilli powder
1 tsp turmeric powder
2 tsp garam masala
1 tsp garlic powder
1 tsp ginger powder
3 green chillies, finely chopped
600ml (1 pt) water
small amount green coriander, chopped

1. Heat the oil in a large pan to a high temperature. Add the onions and cook until they are golden brown.
2. Add the chicken, tomatoes, salt, chilli powder, turmeric powder, garam masala, garlic powder, ginger powder and the green chillies. Stir continuously for about 5 minutes.
3. Cover the pan, reduce the heat and simmer gently for about 25 minutes.
4. Add half of the water to the curry and bring the mixture to the boil. Reduce the heat, cover the pan, and cook for a further 35 minutes, stirring every 10 minutes. Add the remaining water and simmer for a further 45 minutes, stirring every 15 minutes.
5. Transfer the contents to a serving dish, and garnish with the coriander. Serve while hot.
6. The bones are discarded while eating and left on the plate.

CHICKEN BIRYANI

This is a mild rice dish, quick to make and popular with busy cooks. It is usually served with fresh salad. For this recipe you need a wok, or deep frying pan, and a liquidiser.

Cooking and preparation time: 1 hour 20 minutes   *Serves:* 4

25g (1 oz) fresh garlic, peeled
55g (2 oz) fresh ginger, peeled
900ml (1½ pt) chicken stock
170g (6 oz) basmati rice
3 large chicken pieces
120ml (4 fl oz) cooking oil
3 whole cloves
4 whole black peppercorns
½ tsp cumin seeds
½ tsp black mustard seeds
¼ tsp asafoetida
1 medium sized onion, finely chopped
1 tsp tomato purée
85g (3 oz) frozen peas
1 small carrot, sliced thinly
½ tsp turmeric powder
1 tsp salt
½ tsp chilli powder

1. Place the garlic and ginger in a liquidiser and chop finely. Add the contents of the liquidiser to the chicken stock and mix well.
2. Wash the rice like pulses (see page 12).
3. Remove the skin and bones from the chicken and cut the chicken into small pieces, about 7cm (3 in) long.
4. Heat 60ml (2 fl oz) of cooking oil to a high temperature in a wok or deep frying pan; add the chicken pieces and cook over a low heat until the chicken pieces are golden brown.
5. In another separate pan heat the remaining 60ml (2 fl oz) of oil to a high temperature. Add the cloves, peppercorns, cumin, black mustard, and asafoetida and cook for a few seconds. Add the chopped onion, and cook until the onion is golden brown. Add the rice, cooked chicken, tomato purée, peas, carrot, turmeric powder,

(continued overleaf)

salt and chilli powder. Cook for a further 2 minutes, stirring continuously.

6. Add the stock mixture to the rice. Bring it to the boil and reduce the heat. Cover the pan and simmer gently for about 15 minutes. The rice should now look pretty dry.

7. Transfer the contents to a serving dish and serve while hot.

8. The cloves and peppercorns are discarded while eating and left on the plate.

CHICKEN VINDALOO

This is a very hot chicken and potato curry usually served with rice, chapattis or parathas. For this recipe you need a liquidiser and a chopper.

Cooking and preparation time: 1 hour 50 minutes   *Serves:* 4

450g (1 lb) potatoes
900g (2 lb) fresh chicken
1 large onion
6 green chillies
10g (½ oz) fresh ginger
10g (½ oz) fresh garlic
60ml (2 fl oz) cooking oil
3 tsp tomato purée
2 tsp turmeric powder
2 tsp chilli powder
1 tsp garlic powder
1 tsp ginger powder
2 tsp salt
2 tsp garam masala
2 tsp tandoori powder
150ml (5 fl oz) water
small amount green coriander, chopped

1. Peel the potatoes and cut into medium-large cubes about 2.5cm (1 in) square.

2. Remove the skin from the chicken pieces and chop the chicken into small (8cm (3 in) long) pieces.
3. Place the onion, chillies, ginger and garlic in a liquidiser and process until finely chopped.
4. Heat the oil to a high temperature in a large pan. Add the processed onions, chillies, ginger and garlic and cook, stirring continuously, until the onion is golden brown.
5. Add the tomato purée, turmeric powder, chilli powder, garlic powder, ginger powder, salt, garam masala, tandoori powder and the chicken. Mix well, lower the heat and simmer gently for about 10 minutes, stirring every 2–3 minutes.
6. Add the water and let the chicken simmer for about 20 minutes, stirring every 5–7 minutes.
7. Add the potatoes and simmer for another 20 minutes, stirring every 5–7 minutes.
8. Transfer the contents to a serving dish and garnish with green coriander.
9. The bones are discarded while eating and left on the plate.

FRIED CHICKEN CURRY

This is a mouth-watering chicken curry, and is fairly simple to cook. It is usually served with chapattis, rice, noodles or even with chips or mashed potatoes. For this recipe you need either a meat cleaver or a very sharp knife, and a wok or deep frying pan.

Cooking and preparation time: 1 hour 20 minutes   *Serves:* 4

900g (2 lb) chicken pieces
600ml (1 pt) cooking oil (for deep frying)
60ml (2 fl oz) cooking oil
3 large onions, finely chopped
1 tsp chilli powder
1 tsp garam masala
6 green chillies, finely chopped
1 tsp garlic powder

(continued overleaf)

2 tsp tandoori masala
1 tsp turmeric powder
1 tsp salt
4 tsp soy sauce
2 tsp tomato purée
300ml (½ pt) water
small amount green coriander, chopped

1. Remove the skin from the chicken pieces, and chop the chicken into smaller pieces, about 7cm (3 in) long. The bones are left in the chicken pieces.

2. Heat the 600ml (1 pt) of cooking oil in a wok or deep frying pan to a high temperature. Deep fry all the chicken pieces, about 4–5 at a time, until they are golden brown.

3. Heat the 60ml (2 fl oz) of oil in another pan and fry the chopped onions until they are golden brown. Add the chilli powder, garam masala, green chillies, garlic powder, tandoori masala, turmeric powder, salt, soy sauce, and tomato purée. Mix well and cook for about 1–2 minutes.

4. Add the fried chicken, mix well and cook for a further 2–3 minutes, stirring continuously. Add the water, stir, and bring the mixture to the boil. Reduce the heat, cover the pan and simmer gently for a further 15 minutes.

5. Transfer the curry to a serving dish and garnish with the green coriander.

6. The bones are discarded while eating and left on the plate.

TANDOORI CHICKEN

A common dish in Indian restaurants, this is rich flavoured and dry.
It can also be served as a starter or as a side dish with a main course.
Serve with lemon wedges, salad and/or Chinese-style Rice (page
85).

Cooking and preparation time: 3 hours   *Serves:* 4–6

6 chicken pieces (thighs, quarters or legs)
150g (5 fl oz) carton of plain yoghurt
4 tsp garlic, crushed
4 tsp ginger, grated
5 tsp tandoori powder
1 tsp chilli powder
1 tsp oil
salt to taste

1. Make small slits in the chicken pieces and marinade them in a
thick paste made up of all the above ingredients for at least 2 hours,
or preferably overnight.
2. Place the chicken pieces on a baking tray and cook in a pre-
heated oven at 180°C (350°F), gas mark 4, for 50 minutes or until
the chicken is cooked.
3. Then grill the pieces under a hot grill until they turn red.

ROASTED SPICY CHICKEN

This is a 'Sunday roast' with a bit of spice! Serve as a side dish with Peas and Potato Pilau (page 86) or simply with a baked potato and plain yoghurt.

Cooking and preparation time: 1 hour 50 minutes   *Serves:* 4–6

2 tbsp oil
2 tsp garlic, crushed
2 tsp ginger, grated
2 tsp tomato purée
150g (5 oz) tomatoes, peeled and chopped
2 tsp coriander powder
¼ tsp turmeric powder
½ tsp chilli powder
1 tsp garam masala
2 tsp salt (or to taste)
1.35kg (3 lb) whole chicken, with giblets removed
handful of chopped coriander leaves for garnish

1. Heat the oil and add the garlic and ginger and fry for 2 minutes, stirring constantly.
2. Add the tomato purée and cook for another 2 minutes.
3. Then add the tomatoes, powders and salt and cook for 7 minutes, stirring frequently.
4. Make fine slits in the chicken and cover with the sauce.
5. Place the chicken on a baking tray and cook in the oven at 190°C (375°F), gas mark 5, for an hour and a half. The chicken is cooked when a skewer can be easily inserted in the chicken and the juices do not contain any blood.
6. Garnish with the chopped coriander leaves before serving.

SPICY DRUMSTICKS

These are spicy chicken drumsticks which are deep fried until golden brown. They can also be served hot as a starter or as an accompaniment with Chinese-style Rice (page 85).

Cooking and preparation time: 1 hour 30 minutes   *Serves:* 6

12 chicken drumsticks
4 tsp garlic, crushed
2 tsp ginger, grated
4 cloves
4 black peppercorns
2.5cm (1 in) cinnamon stick
3 cardamom pods
1 tsp cumin seeds
1 tsp turmeric powder
1 tsp chilli powder
2 tsp salt (or to taste)
500ml (1 pt) water

For the coating
150g (5 oz) plain flour (and more if required)
1 tsp garam masala
¼ tsp turmeric powder
½ tsp chilli powder
½ tsp salt
3 eggs
oil for deep frying

1. Put the chicken drumsticks in a large saucepan with all the ingredients (*except* the batter mixture), bring to the boil, cover and simmer for 40 minutes.
2. *For the coating:* mix the plain flour with the garam masala, turmeric powder, chilli powder and salt in a deep bowl.
3. Whisk the eggs in a separate bowl.
4. Heat the oil in a large saucepan, coat the chicken drumsticks with the whisked egg, dip into the flour mixture and deep fry until golden brown. Drain on kitchen paper towels.

147

FISH SAK

A very delicious, full flavoured dry curry, that does not mask the flavour of the fish. Serve hot as a main course with chapattis.

Cooking and preparation time: 2 hours 10 minutes   *Serves:* 4

1kg (2 lb 2 oz) fish fillets, steaks or strips

For marinade
4 tbsp coriander powder
1 tsp salt
juice of ½ lemon
1 tsp chilli powder

For frying
oil for deep frying
3 medium sized potatoes, cut into thick chips

For sauce
3 tbsp oil
4 cloves
4 black peppercorns
1 large onion, sliced
2 tsp garlic, crushed
2 tsp ginger, finely grated
2 tbsp tomato purée
2 whole green chillies (optional)
400g (14 oz) tomatoes, peeled and chopped
3 tsp coriander powder
¼ tsp turmeric powder
chilli powder to taste
salt to taste
water
fresh chopped coriander for garnish

1. Marinade the fish in a thick paste made of the coriander powder, salt, lemon juice and chilli powder for at least 40 minutes or overnight for the best result.
2. Deep fry the fish until golden brown and drain on kitchen paper towels or grill under a hot grill until golden brown.
3. Deep fry the chipped potatoes until golden brown and drain on kitchen paper towels.

4. To make the sauce heat the oil, add the cloves, peppercorns and onion. When the onion has browned add the garlic, ginger, tomato purée, green chillies, tomatoes, coriander powder, turmeric powder, chilli powder and salt to taste.

5. Stir and add drops of water to make the sauce into dropping consistency.

6. Let the sauce simmer on low heat for 20 minutes and keep stirring frequently.

7. Lay the fish and potato chips in an ovenproof dish and pour over the sauce.

8. Garnish with the chopped coriander.

9. Heat through in a moderately hot oven at 180°C (350°F), gas mark 4, before serving.

Note: always wash hands thoroughly after handling chillies.

PRAWN SAK

This is a strong flavoured dish, where the flavour of the prawns and the sauce should come through. Serve with a pulse dish, chapattis and rice as a main course.

Cooking and preparation time: 40 minutes   *Serves:* 4–6

2 tbsp oil
1 small onion, sliced
2 tsp garlic, crushed
1 tsp tomato purée
50g (2 oz) tomatoes, peeled and chopped
1 tsp coriander powder
¼ tsp turmeric powder
½ tsp chilli powder
200g (7 oz) prawns, peeled
salt to taste
water as required

1. Heat the oil and fry the onion until golden brown.

(continued overleaf)

2. Then add the garlic and tomato purée and fry for 3 minutes.
3. Now add the rest of the ingredients, stir, cover and simmer for 30 minutes.
4. Add drops of water if the sauce becomes too dry.

FISH PILAU

Savoury rice, great as a main meal or even for a buffet. Serve as a main course with Chilli Salad (page 98), raita and pickles.

Cooking and preparation time: 1 hour + pre-soaking time

Serves: 4–6

450g (1 lb) rice, washed and soaked for 40 minutes
3 tbsp oil
1 large onion, sliced
2 tsp cumin seeds
3 cardamom pods
2 × 2.5cm (1 in) cinnamon sticks
8 cloves
8 black peppercorns
4 tsp garlic, crushed
4 tsp ginger, grated
4 green chillies, whole or chopped
4 medium fish steaks, cut into chunks
115g (4 oz) prawns, peeled
150g (5 oz) tomatoes, peeled and chopped
6 small potatoes, peeled and cut into quarters
250ml (½ pt) water
handful of chopped coriander leaves
salt to taste
25g (1 oz) butter or margarine

1. Wash and soak the rice.
2. Heat the oil and add the onion, cumin seeds, cardamom pods, cinnamon, cloves and peppercorns.

3. When the onion has softened, add the garlic, ginger and chillies and fry for 2 minutes.
4. Then add the fish, prawns, tomatoes, rice, potatoes and water, along with the chopped coriander leaves and salt to taste.
5. Bring to the boil and then cover and simmer on low heat for 40 minutes until the rice has cooked.
6. Add the butter or margarine in blobs, while hot.

Note: to prevent rice from going mushy, never stir while it is cooking. Wash hands thoroughly after handling chillies.

STUFFED MACKEREL CURRY

Spiced and stuffed mackerel is tasty and makes a good change from meat curries. It is usually served with fried rice and can be served with salad as a starter. For this recipe you need a liquidiser.

Cooking and preparation time: 8 hours 30 minutes   *Serves:* 4

25g (1 oz) fresh garlic, peeled
25g (1 oz) fresh ginger, peeled
6 green chillies
2 tsp tomato purée
30ml (1 fl oz) natural yoghurt
½ tsp salt
½ tsp turmeric powder
½ tsp coriander powder
½ tsp cumin powder
1 tsp lemon juice
4 small fresh mackerel (about 450g (1 lb) in total)
60ml (2 fl oz) cooking oil
small amount green coriander, chopped

1. Place the garlic, ginger, chillies, tomato purée, yoghurt, salt, turmeric powder, coriander powder, cumin powder, and lemon juice in a liquidiser and blend into a thickish paste.

(continued overleaf)

2. Cut the heads off the mackerel and slice the fish along their tops, on one side only, so as to enable you to remove the bones from their centres. Make sure that you do not cut completely through, and the mackerel are still whole.

3. Place the mackerel under cold running water for about one minute.

4. Carefully lay the four mackerel out in a large pan and pour the thick paste in the space left by the bones of each of the mackerel. Lift the other half and fold it back so that the blended liquid is in the middle of each of the mackerel.

5. Now leave the fish for about 8 hours.

6. Heat the oil to a high temperature, in a large flat pan. Transfer the fish very carefully to this pan with the hot oil, lower the heat and let it simmer for about 5 minutes. While simmering cover the pan. Turn the fish over carefully, still folded, and cook the other sides by simmering for a further 5 minutes.

7. Transfer the contents to a serving dish and garnish with the coriander. Serve while hot.

COD FISH CURRY

Cod curry is unusual but makes an excellent alternative to meat curries. It can be served with mashed potatoes, chapattis or fried rice. For this recipe you need a liquidiser.

Cooking and preparation time: 40 minutes   *Serves:* 4

10g (½ oz) fresh garlic, peeled
10g (½ oz) fresh ginger, peeled
1 green chilli
225g (8 oz) plum tomatoes, peeled
60ml (2 fl oz) cooking oil
1 large onion, finely chopped
½ tsp turmeric powder
½ tsp chilli powder
½ tsp garam masala
½ tsp salt
675g (1½ lb) cod steaks
small amount green coriander, chopped

1. Blend the garlic, ginger, chilli and tomatoes in a liquidiser, to a thickish paste.
2. Heat the oil to a high temperature in a pan; add the onion and cook until it is golden brown.
3. Add the contents of the liquidiser, turmeric powder, chilli powder, garam masala and salt, and stir continuously for about 2 minutes. Cook this mixture for a further 3 minutes.
4. Arrange the fish steaks in a large casserole and spread the spiced mixture on top of the steaks.
5. Bake the fish and the mixture in a pre-heated oven at 180°C (350°F), gas mark 4, for about 20 minutes.
6. Garnish the fish with fresh green coriander and serve hot.

PRAWN AND PEPPER CURRY

Prawns are rare in Indian homes, but prawn curries do taste good, and are always worth a try. For this recipe you need a deep frying pan or wok.

Cooking and preparation time: 25 minutes   *Serves:* 4

340g (12 oz) green peppers
60ml (2 fl oz) cooking oil
2 medium size onions, finely chopped
2 ripe tomatoes, cut into small pieces
1 tsp salt
½ tsp turmeric powder
½ tsp chilli powder
½ tsp garam masala
340g (12 oz) peeled prawns

1. Chop the peppers lengthways into pieces about 2.5cm (1 in) long and 1cm (½ in) wide.
2. Heat the oil in a large wok, add the onions and fry them until they are golden brown. Add the tomatoes, salt, turmeric powder, chilli powder and garam masala. Cook for a further 2 minutes.
3. Add the peppers and prawns and stir well. Reduce the heat, cover the wok and cook on a very low heat for a further 15 minutes, stirring every 3–4 minutes.
4. Transfer the contents to a serving dish and serve hot.

DRY BHOONA MUSHROOM AND PRAWN CURRY

This is a very mild prawn curry usually served as a side dish with meat curry. For this recipe you need a liquidiser.

Cooking and preparation time: 20 minutes   *Serves:* 4

10g (½ oz) fresh garlic
10g (½ oz) fresh ginger
4 green chillies
60ml (2 fl oz) cooking oil
1 large onion, finely chopped
1 tsp tomato purée
½ tsp salt
½ tsp turmeric powder
½ tsp chilli powder
½ tsp coriander powder
½ tsp cumin powder
225g (8 oz) mushrooms, cut into halves
110g (4 oz) peeled prawns
small amount green coriander, chopped
55g (2 oz) fresh tomatoes, cut into rings

1. Place the garlic, ginger and green chillies in a liquidiser, and chop finely.
2. Heat the oil to a high temperature, in a pan. Add the onion, stir continuously and cook until golden brown. Add the contents of the liquidiser, tomato purée, salt, turmeric powder, chilli powder, coriander powder and cumin powder. Cook the mixture for a further minute, stirring continuously.
3. Add the mushrooms and prawns. Mix well, lower the heat, cover the pan and simmer gently for about 8 minutes, stirring every 2–3 minutes.
4. Transfer the contents to a serving dish and garnish with the green coriander and tomatoes.

TANDOORI FISH

Serve as a starter or as a main course with chipped potatoes and salad.

Cooking and preparation time: 2 hours 40 minutes   *Serves:* 6

6 fish steaks
3 tbsp tandoori powder
150g (5 fl oz) carton plain yoghurt
3 tsp crushed garlic
3 tsp grated ginger
1 tsp salt
juice of one lemon
1 tsp chilli powder

1. Marinade the fish for at least 2 hours, or preferably overnight, in a mixture made of the above ingredients.
2. Cook in a pre-heated oven at 190°C (375°F), gas mark 5, for 40 minutes until the fish has cooked.

Note: the fish has to be cooked on a flat baking tray for the tandoori colour and flavour to come through.

KOORI FISH

This is a quicker way of cooking fish, with a slightly different flavour. Serve with some fried chipped potatoes and salad or with a pulse dish, chapattis and rice.

Cooking and preparation time: 40 minutes   *Serves:* 6

3 tbsp oil
3 tsp coriander powder
1 tsp cumin powder
½ tsp turmeric powder
½ tsp chilli powder
2 tsp garlic, crushed

156

1 tsp ginger, grated
2 whole chillies
2 tsp tomato purée
150g (5 oz) peeled, chopped tomatoes
6 fish steaks
2 tsp salt (or to taste)
water, if necessary
handful of coriander leaves, chopped for garnish

1. Heat the oil in a saucepan, add the powders and fry for 3 minutes, stirring frequently.
2. Add the rest of the ingredients (*except* the water and coriander leaves), stir for 2 minutes, cover and cook on low heat for 30 minutes until the fish flakes off easily. If it begins to dry out before the fish is done, add a drop of water to aid the cooking.
3. Garnish with the chopped coriander leaves before serving.

MAYAI SAK

Plain and simple egg curry. Serve as a main course with chapattis and rice.

Cooking and preparation time: 50 minutes   *Serves:* 6

2 tbsp oil
4 cloves
4 cardamom pods, opened
2.5cm (1 in) cinnamon stick
4 black peppercorns
1 medium sized onion, sliced
2 tsp crushed garlic
2 tbsp tomato purée
150g (5 oz) peeled, chopped tomatoes
2 tsp coriander powder
½ tsp turmeric powder
½ tsp chilli powder

(continued overleaf)

6 hard boiled eggs
4 medium sized potatoes, peeled and quartered
salt to taste
handful of coriander leaves, chopped for garnish

1. Heat the oil and add the whole spices and onion.
2. When the onion has browned, add the garlic and tomato purée and fry for 2 minutes.
3. Then add the rest of the ingredients (*except* for the coriander leaves), stir, cover and simmer for 40 minutes.
4. Garnish with chopped coriander leaves before serving.

KHEEMA MAYAI

This is a versatile dish, made with minced meat and eggs, eaten either as a main course or for brunch! Serve hot with parathas.

Cooking and preparation time: 1 hour 10 minutes   *Serves:* 4

2 tbsp oil
2 cloves
2 black peppercorns
1cm (½ in) cinnamon stick
1 large onion, sliced
2 tsp garlic, crushed
200g (7 oz) mince
1 tbsp tomato purée
115g (4 oz) peeled, chopped tomatoes
2 tsp garam masala
1 tsp coriander powder
½ tsp chilli powder
125ml (¼ pt) water
4 eggs
salt to taste

1. Heat the oil and add the whole spices and onion.

2. When the onion has browned, add the garlic and mince and fry for 10 minutes.

3. Then add the rest of the ingredients (*except* the eggs), stir, cover and simmer for 20 minutes.

4. Transfer into an ovenproof dish and crack the eggs onto the mixture. Cook in a pre-heated oven at 190°C (375°F), gas mark 5, for a further 30 minutes, until the eggs have cooked.

EGG AND POTATO CURRY

This is a mild curry not usually served in restaurants. It can be served with rice or chapattis.

Cooking and preparation time: 45 minutes   *Serves:* 4

6 eggs
225g (8 oz) potatoes
30ml (1 fl oz) cooking oil
1 onion, finely chopped
115g (4 oz) plum tomatoes, peeled
1 tsp salt
1 tsp turmeric powder
1 tsp garam masala
½ tsp chilli powder
½ tsp tandoori masala
1 tsp cumin powder
150ml (5 fl oz) water
small amount green coriander, chopped

1. Hard boil the eggs and remove the shells. Cut the eggs into halves.

2. Peel the potatoes and cut into small pieces, about 1cm (½ in) cubes.

3. Heat the oil to a high temperature in a pan. Add the onion and cook until the onion is golden brown, stirring continuously.

4. Add the tomatoes and cook for about a further 2 minutes stirring

(continued overleaf)

continuously. Now add the salt, turmeric powder, garam masala, chilli powder, tandoori masala and cumin powder. Cook for a further 1 minute.

5. Add the potatoes, mix well, and cook for about 2 minutes stirring continuously. Now add the eggs and cook for about 3–4 minutes.

6. Add the water; bring it to the boil; lower the heat and let it simmer for about 20 minutes, stirring every 5–7 minutes.

7. Transfer the contents to a serving dish and garnish with the coriander.

SCRAMBLED EGGS

A very simple, tasty, quick and easy-to-make dish. Serve with naan bread as a quick snack or for breakfast with parathas or puris.

Cooking and preparation time: 20 minutes   *Serves:* 4

½ tbsp oil
1 small onion, sliced
1 tsp black mustard seeds
6 eggs, whisked
¼ tsp turmeric powder
¼ tsp salt
¼ tsp chilli powder

1. Heat the oil and fry the onion, until soft.
2. Add the mustard seeds and when they start to pop add the rest of the ingredients and stir vigorously until the eggs have scrambled.

Note: make sure the heat is on low when adding mustard seeds, as they are likely to pop.

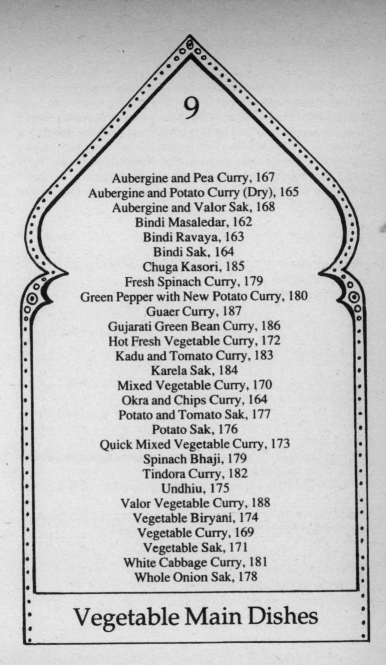

9

Vegetable Main Dishes

BINDI MASALEDAR
okra in a sauce

Bindi or *okra* is also sometimes known as ladies' fingers because of its long slender appearance. It is now available from most large supermarkets. Cook this vegetable without water as water makes it sticky and unappetising. The lid should be left off the pan during most of the cooking time to avoid condensation falling back into the pan causing the contents to go sticky. It should be cooked until tender and slightly crisp. Add some natural yoghurt in the last 5 minutes to make a tangy sauce. Serve this dish with plain boiled rice (page 84).

Cooking and preparation time: 45 minutes   *Serves:* 3–4

450g (1 lb) okra
5 tbsp cooking oil
1 tsp cumin seeds
1 tsp salt
1 tsp ground turmeric
1½ tsp chilli powder
400ml (¾ pint) natural yoghurt

1. Wash the okra and dry very well on a clean tea towel. Top and tail, then slice into 0.5cm (¼ in) thick rings.
2. Heat the oil in a heavy pan, add the cumin seeds and sizzle, covered, for a few seconds. Add the prepared okra, salt and turmeric and toss.
3. Cover and cook for 5 minutes over a medium heat. Stir, add the chilli powder and reduce the heat.
4. Cook without the lid for 30 minutes, or until the okra is tender and not so sticky.
5. Add the yoghurt, bring to the boil and simmer for 5 minutes. Taste and add more salt and chilli powder if needed.

BINDI RAVAYA
stuffed okra

As this dish has no sauce of its own, it is usually served with Kadhi
and plain boiled rice (see pages 56 and 84). For a dinner party you
may wish to serve it alongside a yoghurt dish, such as Cucumber
Raita (page 243).

Cooking and preparation time: 20 minutes   *Serves:* 3–4

450g (1 lb) okra
1 tsp salt
1 tsp chilli powder
1 tsp ground turmeric
4 tbsp ground coriander
8 tbsp cooking oil

1. Wash the okra and dry very well on a clean tea towel. Top and
tail, then split lengthways on one side only.
2. Mix the salt and all the spices together in a bowl using 4 tbsp of
the oil to make the masala stuffing and use it to stuff the okra
lightly.
3. Heat the remaining oil in a frying pan and add the prepared okra.
Lower the heat and cook, covered, until tender. Remove the lid,
turn the heat up slightly and cook, stirring, until crisp on the
outside.

BINDI SAK

This okra dish is served with plain rice, Kadhi and chapattis (pages 84, 56 and 71) for a main meal. To serve it for a light supper, simply roll it in chapattis and top with Cucumber Raita (page 243).

Cooking and preparation time: 20–25 minutes   *Serves:* 2–3

450g (1 lb) okra
4 tbsp cooking oil
1 tsp fenugreek seeds
1 tsp salt
1 tsp ground turmeric
1 tsp chilli powder
1 tbsp ground coriander
1 tsp granulated sugar

1. Wash the okra and dry very well on a clean tea towel. Top and tail, then slice into thick rings. Heat the oil in a frying pan and sizzle the fenugreek seeds in the hot oil for a few seconds.
2. Add the okra, salt, turmeric, chilli powder, coriander, and sugar. Mix well and cook, covered, for 2 minutes.
3. Lower the heat to medium and cook, uncovered, for 15 minutes or until tender and not sticky. Stir occasionally during cooking time.

OKRA AND CHIPS CURRY

Okra, or ladies' fingers, is a very popular vegetable in Indian homes, and since most people like potatoes, okra and chips make an attractive combination.

Cooking and preparation time: 25 minutes   *Serves:* 4

225g (8 oz) fresh okra
60ml (2 fl oz) cooking oil
3 large onions, finely chopped
½ tsp salt

½ tsp turmeric powder
½ tsp chilli powder
½ tsp garam masala
½ tsp tomato purée
115g (4 oz) fried potato chips
1 fresh tomato, cut into small pieces

1. Wash the okra and then dry each piece individually with kitchen roll paper. This is extremely important as okra must be as dry as possible.
2. Cut the okra into 1cm (½ in) long pieces lengthways.
3. Heat the oil to a high temperature in a wok or deep frying pan. Add the onions and the okra. Stir, reduce the heat, cover the pan and let the okra and onions cook for about 10 minutes, stirring every 3–4 minutes.
4. Now add the salt, turmeric powder, chilli powder, garam masala and tomato purée. Mix well and let it cook for a further 3–4 minutes.
5. Add the chips, mix well and let it cook for another 3–4 minutes.
6. Transfer the contents to a serving dish and garnish with the tomato.

AUBERGINE AND POTATO CURRY (DRY)

This is a mild vegetable curry, especially good when served with a meat dish. It is also excellent for vegetarians. It is usually served with rice or chapattis. Parsley or fresh coriander can be used for garnishing.

Cooking and preparation time: 35 minutes   *Serves:* 4

450g (1 lb) potatoes
1 large aubergine approx 225g (8 oz)
2 large onions
60ml (2 fl oz) cooking oil
½ tsp cumin seeds

(continued overleaf)

½ tsp black mustard seeds
2 tsp tomato purée
1 tsp salt
½ tsp turmeric powder
½ tsp chilli powder
1 tsp tandoori masala
1 tsp garam masala
90ml (3 fl oz) water
fresh parsley or green fresh coriander, finely chopped

1. Peel the potatoes and cut them into large chips.
2. Remove the stalk and cut the aubergine into large chip type pieces also.
3. Chop the onions into small pieces.
4. Heat the oil to a high temperature, in a large pan. Add the cumin and mustard seeds to the oil and cook until they are golden brown. This will only take a few seconds.
5. Add the chopped onions. Cook together until the onions are golden brown. Add the tomato purée, salt, turmeric powder, chilli powder, tandoori masala, garam masala, potatoes and aubergine pieces. Stir and cook for another few minutes. Reduce the heat.
6. Add the water; bring to the boil, cover the pan and simmer gently for about 30–35 minutes, stirring every 5–7 minutes. Switch off the heat and place the cooked curry in a serving dish.
7. Garnish with parsley or fresh coriander.

AUBERGINE AND PEA CURRY

The dark skin of the aubergine contrasts very well with the peas in this dish and is good served at a dinner party with puris, Mixed Vegetable Rice and Tarka Dhal (see pages 74, 88 and 195). More simply, you could serve it with plain rice or chapattis (pages 84 and 71).

Cooking and preparation time: 25–30 minutes   *Serves:* 4–6

1 large aubergine
225g (8 oz) frozen peas
4 tbsp cooking oil
1 tsp mustard seeds
1 tsp cumin seeds
1½ tsp salt
½ tsp ground turmeric
1 tsp chilli powder
2 tbsp ground coriander
½ cup water – if necessary
225g (8 oz) can tomatoes

1. Wash and cut the aubergine into large chunks and halve the potatoes. Heat the oil in a heavy based pan, add the mustard and cumin seeds and cover for a few seconds until the 'popping' has stopped. Add the aubergine, salt and turmeric.
2. Mix well, reduce the heat and cook, covered, for 2 minutes. Add the peas, chilli powder and coriander, stir and cook, covered, for 15 minutes or until the vegetables are tender.
3. Add ½ cup of water if necessary, but if the aubergine is fresh it should not be necessary to add any water.
4. Chop the tomatoes and add to the pan. Cook for another 5 minutes.

AUBERGINE AND VALOR SAK

Valor is a type of bean and can be found at Indian grocery shops. Do make sure that they are fresh as this dish is cooked with little or no water and when the vegetables are fresh they give out their own juices. If the heat is kept very low, these juices are usually enough to cook the dish.

Serve on a freshly made paratha, topped with Cucumber Raita (page 243), or with rice or chapattis.

Cooking and preparation time: 50 minutes   *Serves:* 4

450g (1 lb) green valor beans (available at most Indian grocers)
1 large aubergine
5 tbsp cooking oil
1 tsp mustard seeds
1 tsp cumin seeds
1 tsp ground turmeric
1½ tsp salt
1½ tsp chilli powder
2 tbsp ground coriander
1 tsp granulated sugar
water
3 tomatoes

1. Wash the valor beans and prepare by snapping off the tips and pulling off strings along both sides of the bean. Pull the beans open and cut in half lengthwise. Wash the aubergine and cut into large chunks.
2. Heat the oil in a heavy based pan, add the black mustard and cumin seeds. Cover the pan for a few seconds until the seeds have all 'popped'.
3. Add the drained aubergine and valor beans, mix with a wooden spoon, add the turmeric and salt and cook, covered, over very low heat for 10 minutes.
4. Add the chilli powder, sugar and a sprinkling of water if required. Continue cooking over low heat until the vegetables are tender (about 30 minutes).
5. Chop the tomatoes and spread over the vegetables and cook for a further 5 minutes. Stir very carefully and serve.

VEGETABLE CURRY

Vegetable curry is ideal to serve at a dinner party. Either serve it with Plain Parathas (page 78), or with Matar-bhaat (page 95). Green Coriander and Coconut Chutney (page 234) goes very well with it. You could also buy a jar of mango pickles, available from Indian grocery shops, for a final touch.

Cooking and preparation time: 40–45 minutes   *Serves:* 4

5 tbsp cooking oil
2 cloves
2.5cm (1 in) cinnamon stick
3 black peppercorns
1 large onion, chopped
400g (14 oz) can tomatoes
2 tbsp tomato purée
1½ tsp salt
1 tsp ground turmeric
2 tbsp ground coriander
1 tsp chilli powder
1 large potato
2 medium sized carrots
1½ cups hot water
125g (4 oz) frozen peas

1. Heat the oil in a heavy based pan, add the cloves, cinnamon stick, black peppercorns and onion and cook for 5 minutes.
2. Chop or liquidise the tomatoes and add to the pan. Cook for a further 2 minutes. Add the tomato purée, salt, turmeric, coriander and chilli powder and cook for 3 minutes.
3. Cut the potato and carrots into large chunks and add to the pan. Cook, covered, for 5 minutes over medium heat.
4. Add the water and cook for 15 minutes. Add the peas towards the last 5 minutes of cooking time.

Variation: Hard boil 4 eggs, and at the end of the cooking as above, cut them into two, lengthways, and add to the curry. Sprinkle with garam masala and mix gently, being careful not to break up the vegetables.

MIXED VEGETABLE CURRY

This is a good supper dish. Serve it on a bed of plain boiled rice or with Plain Parathas (pages 84 and 78). Care should be taken when stirring as the vegetables break up easily and you will be left with a pot of mush!

Cooking and preparation time: 30 minutes   *Serves:* 6–8

6 tbsp cooking oil
2.5cm (1 in) cinnamon stick
3 cloves
2 black peppercorns
2 cardamom pods
1 large onion, sliced
2 cloves garlic, crushed
5 small potatoes, peeled and halved
3 carrots, peeled and cut into 2.5cm (1 in) squares
2 tsp salt
1 tsp ground turmeric
½ cauliflower, divided into florets
1 green pepper, deseeded and cut into 2.5cm (1 in) squares
2 tsp chilli powder
2 tbsp ground coriander
1 tsp granulated sugar
1 cup water
400g (14 oz) can tomatoes
3 tbsp tomato purée
125g (4 oz) frozen peas
½ tsp garam masala

1. Heat the oil in a heavy pan and add the cinnamon stick, cloves, black peppercorns, cardamom pods, onion and garlic. Stir fry for 1 minute, then add the potatoes, carrots, salt and turmeric and mix well.
2. Reduce the heat, cover and cook for 10 minutes, stirring occasionally. Add the cauliflower, green pepper, chilli powder, coriander, sugar and water and cook, covered, for 5 minutes.
3. Add the tomatoes, tomato purée and peas and cook for another 10 minutes. If there is excess liquid left in the pan, boil away with lid off until the sauce is quite thick and coats the vegetables in the pan.
4. Sprinkle with garam masala and serve hot.

VEGETABLE SAK

A vegetarian's delight of a very simple sauce transforming vegetables such as cauliflower or aubergines and potatoes, chick peas, courgettes, mixed vegetables, or any other combination you care to choose, into a main course. Serve with chapattis, parathas, puris and/or rice.

Cooking and preparation time: 40 minutes   *Serves:* 4–6

2 tbsp oil
1 tsp black mustard seeds
3 tsp garlic, crushed
1 tsp ginger, grated
1 tbsp tomato purée
150g (5 oz) tomatoes, peeled and chopped
2 tsp coriander powder
¼ tsp turmeric powder
½ tsp chilli powder
500g (1 lb 2 oz) vegetables of your choice, chopped
salt to taste
125ml (¼ pt) water
coriander leaves for garnish

1. Heat the oil, turn the heat to low and add the mustard seeds.
2. When the mustard seeds start to pop, add the garlic and ginger and stir for 2 minutes.
3. Add the tomato purée and cook for 1 minute, before adding the rest of the ingredients (*except* for the water and coriander leaves). Stir together.
4. Add the water, cover and simmer on low heat for 25–30 minutes, until the vegetables have cooked. (It may be necessary to add more water while cooking the vegetables.)
5. Garnish with chopped coriander leaves before serving.

Note: make sure the heat is on low when adding mustard seeds, as they are likely to pop.

HOT FRESH VEGETABLE CURRY

This is a very hot vegetable curry usually served with rice. For this recipe you need a liquidiser.

Cooking and preparation time: 45 minutes   *Serves:* 4

340g (12 oz) potatoes
1 large aubergine approx 225g (8 oz)
115g (4 oz) plum tomatoes, peeled
25g (1 oz) fresh garlic, peeled
55g (2 oz) fresh ginger, peeled
60ml (2 fl oz) cooking oil
½ tsp cumin seeds
½ tsp black mustard seeds
½ tsp turmeric powder
1 tsp garam masala
1½ tsp salt
¾ tsp chilli powder
8 green chillies, chopped
170g (6 oz) frozen peas (thawed)
600ml (1 pt) water
small portion of fresh green coriander

1. Peel the potatoes and cut them into 2.5cm (1 in) cubes.
2. Remove the stalk of the aubergine and cut into 2.5cm (1 in) cubes.
3. Place the tomatoes, garlic, and ginger into a liquidiser and blend into a thickish paste.
4. Heat the oil to a high temperature, in a pan. Add the cumin and mustard seeds and leave it cooking for a few seconds. Add the thick paste, turmeric powder, garam masala, salt, chilli powder, potatoes, aubergine, green chillies and peas. Stir continuously and cook for about 5 minutes.
5. Add the water, bring it to the boil and simmer gently for about 30 minutes.
6. Place the curry in a serving dish and garnish with fresh coriander.

QUICK MIXED VEGETABLE CURRY

If you are in a hurry, then this curry is ideal. It does not take too long to cook, and can be served with plain boiled rice. It is also good served with bread, or chapattis.

Cooking and preparation time: 30 minutes   *Serves:* 4

45ml (1½ fl oz) cooking oil
½ tsp cumin seeds
½ tsp black mustard seeds
1 large onion, finely chopped
2 tsp tomato purée
1 tsp turmeric powder
1 tsp chilli powder
1 tsp garam masala
1 tsp salt
1 tsp garlic powder
450g (1 lb) frozen, mixed vegetables
2 small potatoes, chopped into very small pieces
300ml (½ pt) water

1. Heat the oil to a high temperature in a pan, and add the cumin, black mustard and chopped onion. Cook together until the onion is golden brown.
2. Add the tomato purée, turmeric powder, chilli powder, garam masala, salt, garlic powder, mixed vegetables and potatoes. Stir continuously and cook for a further 5 minutes.
3. Add the water to the vegetables, and bring to the boil. Reduce the heat and simmer gently for about 20 minutes.
4. Serve hot.

VEGETABLE BIRYANI

If you like rice and are a vegetarian, then vegetable biryani is just the thing for you. It is usually served with fresh salad. For this recipe you need a deep frying pan, or wok, and a liquidiser.

Cooking and preparation time: 40 minutes   *Serves:* 4

175g (6 oz) basmati rice
25g (1 oz) fresh garlic, peeled
25g (1 oz) fresh ginger, peeled
60ml (2 fl oz) cooking oil
3 whole cloves
½ tsp cumin seeds
½ tsp black mustard seeds
¼ tsp asafoetida
1 large onion, finely chopped
1 tsp tomato purée
115g (4 oz) frozen peas
170g (6 oz) frozen diced carrots (properly thawed)
225g (8 oz) frozen cauliflower (properly thawed)
1 large potato, finely chopped
½ tsp turmeric powder
1 tsp salt
½ tsp chilli powder
600ml (1 pt) water

1. Wash the rice, like pulses as described in the introduction.
2. Place the garlic and ginger in a liquidiser, and chop finely.
3. Heat the oil to a high temperature in a wok or deep frying pan. Add the cloves, cumin, black mustard and asafoetida, and cook for a few seconds. Add the chopped onion, and cook until the onion is golden brown.
4. Add the contents of the liquidiser and cook for a further 2 minutes. Add the tomato purée, peas, carrots, cauliflower, potato, turmeric powder, salt and chilli powder. Cook for a further 2 minutes, stirring continuously.
5. Add the water and rice. Bring the mixture to the boil and reduce the heat. Cover the pan and simmer gently for about 15 minutes. The rice should now look dry.
6. Transfer the contents to a serving dish and serve while hot.

UNDHIU

This is an all-in-one dish of mixed vegetables. The principle is similar to the French dish ratatouille. All the vegetables are put into a large pot along with all the spices and seasonings and are cooked slowly in their own juices. Serve with chapattis and raita.

Cooking and preparation time: 30–35 minutes   *Serves:* 4

1 medium aubergine
6 small new potatoes
125g (4 oz) mange tout peas
125g (4 oz) frozen peas
2.5cm (1 in) root ginger
25g (1 oz) raw peanuts
1 tsp salt
1 tsp ground turmeric
1½ tsp chilli powder
3 tbsp ground coriander
2 tbsp chopped green coriander
1 tsp granulated sugar
8 tbsp oil

1. Wash and cut the aubergine into fairly large chunks. Scrape and halve the potatoes and top and tail the mange tout peas.
2. Mince the ginger and peanuts together. Add the salt, turmeric, chilli powder, ground and green coriander, sugar and oil. Mix well to form the masala paste. Add to the vegetables and stir to coat all the pieces evenly.
3. Place in a heavy based pan and cook, covered, until the vegetables are tender. Keep the heat to the minimum throughout the cooking time.

POTATO SAK

This is a favourite dish with many families and probably the best way to describe it is to liken it to chips: spicy chips! It is good served with plain boiled rice, Dhal and some freshly made chapattis for a dinner party. Include a yoghurt dish and some mango pickles to complete the meal. A large variety of ready-made pickles is available from Indian grocery shops.

Cooking and preparation time: 15–20 minutes   *Serves:* 4–6

8 tbsp oil
1 tsp mustard seeds
1 tsp cumin seeds
450g (1 lb) potatoes, peeled, halved and sliced
1½ tsp salt
1 tsp ground turmeric
1 tsp chilli powder
1 tbsp ground coriander
1 tsp granulated sugar
1 tbsp green coriander, chopped

1. Heat the oil in a large frying pan, add the black mustard and cumin seeds and close the lid until the 'popping' stops.
2. Add the potato slices, salt, turmeric and mix well. Reduce the heat, add the chilli powder, coriander and sugar, mix to coat all the potato slices, cover and cook for 5–7 minutes or until the potatoes are cooked.
3. Remove the lid, turn up the heat and cook, stirring gently, until crisp and lightly browned.
4. Garnish with coriander.

POTATO AND TOMATO SAK

This is a slightly different flavoured dish from that described under Vegetable Sak (page 171) – but it is equally delicious! Serve hot as a main course with puris or parathas.

Cooking and preparation time: 40 minutes   *Serves:* 4–6

2 tbsp oil
1 tsp mustard seeds
2 tsp garlic, crushed
2 tsp ginger, grated
1 tsp tomato purée
50g (2 oz) tomatoes, peeled and chopped
2 tsp coriander powder
¼ tsp turmeric powder
½ tsp chilli powder
handful coriander leaves, chopped
handful fenugreek leaves, chopped
6 medium sized potatoes, peeled and cut into small cubes
125ml (¼ pt) water
salt to taste

1. Heat the oil and add the mustard seeds. When they start to pop add the rest of the ingredients and stir.
2. Cover and simmer for 30 minutes until the potatoes have softened.

Note: make sure the heat is on low when adding mustard seeds, as they are likely to pop.

WHOLE ONION SAK

It is surprising how this, one of the more common vegetables, is changed into an exotic dish by the use of a few spices. Serve it simply with freshly made chapattis (page 71). It may also be served with parathas or rice (pages 78 and 84).

Cooking and preparation time: 40–45 minutes   *Serves:* 4

450g (1 lb) shallots or small onions, peeled
1cm (½ in) root ginger
1 tsp salt
1 tsp chilli powder
1 tsp ground turmeric
3 tbsp ground coriander
2 tbsp chopped green coriander
1 tsp granulated sugar
8 tbsp oil
water

1. Cut each shallot into four segments lengthways, cutting only three quarters of the way down so that the segments are held together.
2. Mince the ginger finely and add to the salt, chilli powder, turmeric, ground and green coriander, sugar and 2 tbsp of the oil. Mix well to create the masala filling and use it to fill the shallots.
3. In a heavy pan, heat the remainder of the oil and add the prepared shallots. Turn the heat down to minimum and cook, covered, until the shallots are tender. Stir frequently and if the masala begins to stick to the bottom of the pan add a little water, about 2 tbsp at a time.

SPINACH BHAJI

A healthy, delicious dish made with spinach that goes well with the
Khichris. Serve as a main course with either Moong Bean (page 91)
or Dhal Khichri (page 90) and some plain yoghurt.

Cooking and preparation time: 50 minutes   *Serves:* 4–6

2–4 large bunches of spinach
3 tbsp oil
4 tsp garlic, crushed
150g (5 oz) tomatoes, peeled and chopped
½ tsp chilli powder *or* 3 finely chopped green chillies
salt to taste
water, if required

1. Clean the spinach. Spinach contains enough juices to allow it to
cook without needing any extra water. After washing the spinach
thoroughly, mop it dry with kitchen paper towels. Chop the spinach.
2. Heat the oil in a saucepan.
3. Add the garlic and spinach, and then the rest of the ingredients.
4. Stir and add a drop of water if required (not always necessary).
5. Cover and cook on low heat for at least 40 minutes, stirring
occasionally.

FRESH SPINACH CURRY

If you like spinach, then you must try this dish. It can be served
instead of boiled spinach or, like other vegetable curries, with
chapattis or a side dish.

Cooking and preparation time: 25 minutes   *Serves:* 4

60ml (2 fl oz) cooking oil
1 small onion, finely chopped
450g (1 lb) fresh spinach, finely chopped

(continued overleaf)

½ tsp turmeric powder
½ tsp chilli powder
½ tsp salt
½ tsp garam masala
½ tsp garlic powder
1 tsp tomato purée
1 tomato, cut into small pieces

1. Heat the oil to a high temperature, in a large pan. Add the onion and cook until the onion is golden brown. Add the spinach, turmeric powder, chilli powder, salt, garam masala, garlic powder and tomato purée. Mix well, cover the pan, lower the heat, and let it simmer for about 15 minutes, stirring every 4–5 minutes.
2. Transfer the spinach to a serving dish and garnish with the tomato.

GREEN PEPPER WITH NEW POTATO CURRY

This is a very mild vegetable curry and can be served with chapattis, or pulse curries and rice. It tastes especially good with new potatoes, but ordinary potatoes can be used.

Cooking and preparation time: 35 minutes   *Serves:* 4

60ml (2 fl oz) cooking oil
½ tsp cumin seeds
1 onion, finely chopped
225g (8 oz) new potatoes, peeled and cut into very thin discs, like crisps
2 large green peppers, sliced in rings
1 tsp salt
½ tsp turmeric powder
½ tsp garam masala
90ml (3 fl oz) water
1 tsp tomato purée
½ tsp chilli powder

1. Heat the oil to a high temperature in a wok or a deep pan. Add the cumin, cook for a few seconds and add the onion. Cook until golden brown.
2. Add the potatoes, peppers, salt, turmeric powder, garam masala, water, tomato purée, and the chilli powder. Mix well.
3. Bring the water to the boil, lower the heat and cover the pan. Simmer gently for about 20 minutes, stirring every 5–7 minutes.
4. Transfer the contents to a serving dish and serve while hot.

WHITE CABBAGE CURRY

This is a hot vegetable curry usually served with a rice dish, or chapattis. It also makes an excellent filling for toasted sandwiches. For this recipe you need a liquidiser.

Cooking and preparation time: 40 minutes   *Serves:* 4

25g (1 oz) fresh garlic, peeled
55g (2 oz) fresh ginger, peeled
6 whole green chillies
60ml (2 fl oz) cooking oil
½ tsp cumin seeds
½ tsp black mustard seeds
4 whole cloves
4 whole black peppercorns
¼ tsp asafoetida
675g (1½ lb) white cabbage, shredded
2 tsp tomato purée
½ tsp turmeric powder
½ tsp chilli powder
1 tsp garam masala
1 tsp salt
4 tsp soy sauce
180ml (6 fl oz) water

1. Place the garlic, ginger, and green chillies in a liquidiser, and chop finely.

(continued overleaf)

2. Heat the oil to a high temperature in a wok or large pan, and add the cumin, black mustard, whole cloves, whole peppercorns, and asafoetida. Cook for a few seconds.

3. Add the cabbage, tomato purée, turmeric powder, chilli powder, garam masala, salt and soy sauce. Cook for a further few seconds.

4. Add the contents of the liquidiser and water to the cabbage.

5. Stir well and bring the mixture to the boil. Cover the pan, reduce the heat and simmer gently for about 20 minutes, stirring every 5–7 minutes.

6. Transfer the contents to a serving dish and serve hot.

7. The cloves are discarded and left at the side of the plate while eating.

TINDORA CURRY

This is a very unusual curry, and tastes like courgettes or cucumber. If you are prepared to try something new, then this may be to your taste. It is usually served with rice or chapattis. For this recipe you need a liquidiser.

Cooking and preparation time: 20 minutes   *Serves:* 4

85g (3 oz) fresh garlic, peeled
85g (3 oz) fresh ginger, peeled
4 whole green chillies
450g (1 lb) fresh tindora (see Glossary)
60ml (2 fl oz) cooking oil
½ tsp cumin seeds
½ tsp black mustard seeds
¼ tsp asafoetida
2 tsp tomato purée
1 tsp salt
½ tsp turmeric powder
1 tsp chilli powder
1 tsp garam masala
4 tsp soy sauce
300ml (½ pt) water
1 fresh tomato, cut into small pieces for garnishing

1. Place the garlic, ginger, and green chillies into a liquidiser and chop finely.
2. Cut each fresh tindora into four pieces.
3. Heat the oil to a high temperature, in a large pan, and add the cumin, black mustard and asafoetida. Fry for a few seconds.
4. Add the cut tindora, contents of the liquidiser, tomato purée, salt, turmeric powder, chilli powder, garam masala and soy sauce. Stir and cook for about 2 minutes. Add the water, and bring to the boil. Reduce the heat, cover the pan and simmer gently for about 7 minutes.
5. Transfer the contents to a serving dish and garnish with the tomato.

KADU AND TOMATO CURRY

Kadu tastes somewhat similar to marrow. This is a very mild curry usually served with chapattis.

Cooking and preparation time: 25 minutes   *Serves:* 4

225g (8 oz) kadu (see Glossary)
60ml (2 fl oz) cooking oil
½ tsp black mustard seeds
½ tsp cumin seeds
115g (4 oz) fresh tomatoes, finely chopped
½ tsp salt
⅓ tsp turmeric powder
½ tsp garam masala
½ tsp chilli powder

1. Peel the kadu and cut into about 2.5cm (1 in) cubes.
2. Heat the oil to a high temperature, in a large pan. Add the black mustard and cumin seeds and let it cook for a few seconds. Add the tomatoes, salt, turmeric powder, garam masala and chilli powder. Let this spice mixture cook for about 1 minute.
3. Add the kadu. Lower the heat and let the kadu simmer for about 30 minutes, stirring every 5–7 minutes.
4. Transfer the contents to a serving dish. Serve hot.

KARELA SAK

This is quite a strong flavoured green vegetable curry which is normally made in small quantities as a dry dish to be accompanied with wet dishes like Dhal. Serve as a main course with Dhal, chapattis and rice, accompanied with some plain yoghurt.

Cooking and preparation time: 40 minutes   *Serves:* 4

2 karelas (see Glossary)
2 tbsp oil
1 large onion, finely sliced
1 tsp garlic, crushed
1 tsp ginger, grated
2 tsp tomato purée
85g (3 oz) tomatoes, peeled and chopped
1 tsp coriander powder
¼ tsp turmeric powder
chilli powder to taste
salt to taste
water, as required

1. Core the karelas, discard the seeds and slice into fine rings.
2. Heat the oil and fry the karela rings until lightly brown.
3. Next, add the onion and fry until soft and, again, just lightly brown.
4. Add the garlic and ginger, stir and allow to fry for 1 minute.
5. Then add the tomato purée and let it stand in the oil for at least 1 minute before stirring.
6. Finally, add the rest of the ingredients and stir.
7. If the mixture is too dry add a small drop of water, then cover and cook on a low heat for at least 30 minutes, stirring frequently.

CHUGA KASORI

This dish has a very nutty flavour yet the taste of the corn still comes through. It is an unusual but delicious combination of flavours. Serve with chapattis and rice. For this recipe you need a liquidiser.

Cooking and preparation time: 1 hour   *Serves:* 4–6

300g (11 oz) peanuts
250ml (½ pt) water
2 tbsp oil
1 tsp black mustard seeds
3 tsp garlic, crushed
1 tsp ginger, grated
2 tbsp tomato purée
150g (5 oz) tomatoes, peeled and chopped
600g (1 lb 4 oz) sweetcorn
   ***or* 3 sweetcorn cobs cut into 3 pieces each**
1 tsp chilli powder (or to taste)
¼ tsp turmeric powder
2 tsp coriander powder
2 whole green chillies (optional)
salt to taste
fresh coriander leaves, chopped for garnish

1. Liquidise the peanuts into a coarse mixture with 125ml (¼ pt) of the water.
2. Heat the oil in a saucepan and carefully add the mustard seeds.
3. When the seeds start popping, add the garlic and ginger and stir.
4. Add the tomato purée and chopped tomatoes and allow to cook for 2 minutes.
5. Add the rest of the ingredients (*except* the coriander leaves) and stir.
6. Add the remaining water, bring to the boil, lower the heat, cover and simmer for 40 minutes. (It may be necessary to add more water during cooking.)
7. Garnish with chopped coriander leaves before serving.

Note: you can use 3 tbsp peanut butter instead of the liquidised raw peanuts and water.
Make sure the heat is on low when adding mustard seeds, as they are likely to pop.
Wash hands thoroughly after handling chillies.

GUJARATI GREEN BEAN CURRY

Many residents of India are vegetarians and they have therefore improvised on many of the standard pulse and vegetable dishes. Green beans are one of their specialities.

Cooking and preparation time: 15 minutes   *Serves:* 4

60ml (2 fl oz) cooking oil
½ tsp black mustard seeds
½ tsp cumin seeds
¼ tsp asafoetida
55g (2 oz) fresh tomatoes, finely chopped
½ tsp salt
½ tsp turmeric powder
½ tsp cumin powder
½ tsp coriander powder
½ tsp chilli powder
340g (12 oz) frozen green beans (thawed)
120ml (4 fl oz) water

1. Heat the oil to a high temperature, in a large pan. Add the mustard seeds, cumin seeds and asafoetida and let it cook for a few seconds. Add the tomatoes, salt, turmeric powder, cumin powder, coriander powder and chilli powder. Let this spice mixture cook for about 2 minutes.
2. Add the beans, mix well and then add the water. Bring the water to the boil, lower the heat and let the beans simmer for about 8 minutes, stirring every 2–3 minutes.
3. Transfer the contents to a serving dish and serve hot.

GUAER CURRY

It is difficult to describe the flavour of guaer. The closest approximation is that it tastes similar to green beans.

Cooking and preparation time: 45 minutes   *Serves:* 4

225g (8 oz) guaer (see Glossary)
60ml (2 fl oz) cooking oil
½ tsp black mustard seeds
½ tsp cumin seeds
¼ tsp asafoetida
2 tsp tomato purée
1 tsp salt
1 tsp turmeric powder
1 tsp cumin powder
1 tsp coriander powder
1 tsp chilli powder
450ml (15 fl oz) water

1. Top and tail the guaer and then cut into about 2.5cm (1 in) lengths.
2. Heat the oil to a high temperature, in a large pan. Add the black mustard seeds, cumin seeds and asafoetida and let it cook for a few seconds. Add the tomato purée, salt, turmeric powder, cumin powder, coriander powder and chilli powder. Let this spice mixture cook for about 2 minutes.
3. Add the guaer, mix well and then add the water. Lower the heat and let the guaer simmer for about 30 minutes, stirring every 5–6 minutes.
4. Transfer the contents to a serving dish and serve hot.

VALOR VEGETABLE CURRY

This is an unusual vegetable curry and tastes very similar to courgettes. It is usually served with chapattis or with a pulse curry and rice.

Cooking and preparation time: 35 minutes   *Serves:* 4

**2 medium size potatoes
340g (12 oz) fresh valor (see Glossary)
60ml (2 fl oz) cooking oil
1 tsp black mustard seeds
1 tsp cumin seeds
¼ tsp asafoetida
2 tsp tomato purée
½ tsp chilli powder
1 tsp salt
1½ tsp garam masala
½ tsp turmeric powder
1 tsp garlic powder
1 tsp tandoori masala
300ml (½ pt) water
1 fresh tomato, cut into small pieces for garnishing**

1. Peel the potatoes and cut into about 2.5cm (1 in) cubes.
2. Top and tail the valor and cut them lengthways into about 2.5cm (1 in) long pieces.
3. Heat the oil in a wok or pan and add the black mustard, cumin and asafoetida. Cook for a few seconds. Add the potatoes, valor, tomato purée, chilli powder, salt, garam masala, turmeric powder, garlic powder and tandoori masala. Stir continuously and cook for a further 5 minutes.
4. Add the water; bring it to the boil, reduce the heat and simmer gently for a further 20 minutes.
5. Transfer the contents to a serving dish and garnish with the tomato. Serve while hot.

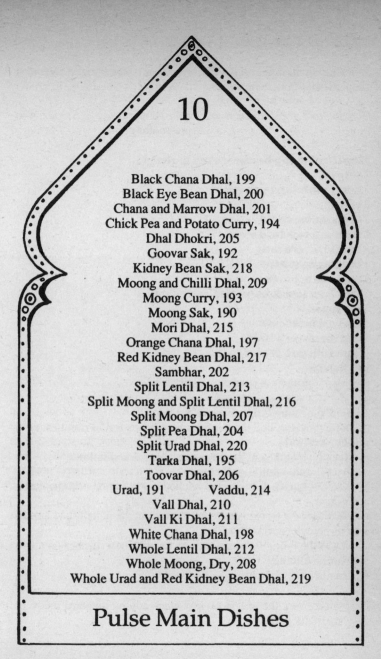

10

Pulse Main Dishes

MOONG SAK

A healthy dish, rich in fibre and very tasty – just try it! Serve with chapattis and rice.

Cooking and preparation time: 1 hour 30 minutes   *Serves:* 4–6
                               + pre-soaking time

150g (5 oz) mung beans, soaked overnight
2 tbsp oil
2.5cm (1 in) cinnamon stick
3 cloves
1 large onion, sliced
1 tsp black mustard seeds
3 tsp garlic, crushed
1 tsp ginger, grated
2 tsp tomato purée
200g (7 oz) tomatoes, peeled and chopped
1 tsp sugar
2 tsp coriander powder
¼ tsp turmeric powder
½ tsp chilli powder (or to taste)
salt to taste
freshly chopped coriander for garnish

1. Soak the mung beans overnight. Drain.
2. In fresh water, boil the soaked mung beans for 50 minutes, until mushy, and drain.
3. Heat the oil and add the cinnamon, cloves and onion.
4. Fry the onion until lightly brown.
5. Add the mustard seeds, and as they begin to pop add the garlic and ginger.
6. Next, add the tomato purée, tomatoes and the rest of the ingredients (*except* the coriander).
7. Stir in the mung beans and allow to boil, then simmer on a low heat for 30 minutes.
8. Garnish with the coriander and serve.

Note: make sure the heat is on low when adding mustard seeds, as they are likely to pop.

URAD

This is a black lentil with its own exceptional taste and this dish does it justice! Serve as a main course with chapattis, rice and raita as an accompaniment.

Cooking and preparation time: 1 hour 30 minutes　　*Serves:* 4–6
　　　　　　　　　　　　　　　　+ pre-soaking time

230g (8 oz) black beans, soaked overnight

For boiling the black beans
500ml (1 pt) water
½ medium sized onion, sliced
2 cloves
2.5cm (1 in) cinnamon stick
1 tsp salt

For the sauce
3 tbsp oil
3 cloves
3 black peppercorns
2.5cm (1 in) cinnamon stick
1 large onion, sliced
3 tsp garlic, crushed
1 tsp ginger, grated
2 tsp tomato purée
150g (5 oz) tomatoes, peeled and chopped
¼ tsp turmeric powder
3 tsp coriander powder
½ tsp chilli powder (or to taste)
1 tsp salt
210ml (7 fl oz) plain yoghurt
250ml (½ pt) water
handful of coriander leaves, chopped, for garnish

1. Soak the black beans overnight. Drain.
2. Boil the beans and the other ingredients listed 'for boiling' in a saucepan for 40 minutes and drain.
3. *For the sauce:* heat the oil in another saucepan, add the whole spices and onion and fry until the onion has browned.

(continued overleaf)

4. Add the garlic and ginger and fry for 2 minutes, stirring frequently.
5. Add the rest of the ingredients (*except* the coriander leaves) and the beans, stir, bring to the boil, cover and simmer for 40 minutes.
6. Garnish with the chopped coriander leaves before serving.

GOOVAR SAK

This is a bean which has a distinct flavour of its own. It is quite a treat! Serve as a main course, with a Dhal dish as an accompaniment, chapattis and rice.

Cooking and preparation time: 50 minutes   *Serves:* 4–6

450g (1 lb) goovar
3 tbsp oil
3 cloves
3 black peppercorns
2.5cm (1 in) cinnamon stick
1 medium sized onion, sliced
2 tsp garlic, crushed
2 tsp tomato purée
85g (3 oz) tomatoes, peeled and chopped
3 tsp coriander powder
¼ tsp turmeric powder
½ tsp chilli powder
1 tsp salt (or to taste)
3 medium sized potatoes, peeled and cut into small cubes
125ml (¼ pt) water

1. To prepare the goovar, nip the ends, break in half and then rinse in water.
2. Heat the oil, add the whole spices and onion and fry until the onion has browned.
3. Add the garlic and tomato purée and fry for 2 minutes, stirring frequently.
4. Add the rest of the ingredients, stir, cover and simmer for 40 minutes until the goovar is tender to touch.

MOONG CURRY

This dish can be served quite thick with chapattis or watery like soup with fresh bread and butter. It is equally delicious served cold with a swirl of yoghurt on a hot summer's day. Mung beans are high in protein and fibre which makes this an ideal dish for someone on a diet.

Cooking and preparation time: 1 hour 25 minutes   *Serves:* 6–8

450g (1 lb) mung beans
1750ml (3½ pts) boiling water
400g (14 oz) can tomatoes
2 green chillies
2.5cm (1 in) root ginger, peeled
3 tbsp cooking oil
1 tsp mustard seeds
3 tsp cumin seeds
2 tsp salt
1 tsp chilli powder
1 tsp ground turmeric
2 tbsp ground coriander
2 tbsp jaggery or brown sugar
juice of 1 lemon
1 tbsp green coriander, chopped, for garnish

1. Wash the mung beans and add to the boiling water in a pan. Boil for 1 hour, adding more boiling water during the cooking time if necessary.
2. Mince together the tomatoes, chillies and ginger. Heat the oil in a heavy based pan, add the mustard and cumin seeds and cover the pan for a few seconds until the 'popping' stops. Add the tomato mixture and bring to the boil. Simmer, covered, for 2 minutes.
3. Add the salt, chilli powder, turmeric, ground coriander, jaggery or brown sugar, and the lemon juice. Mix well and simmer for another 2 minutes.
4. Add the mung beans with all the water they have been cooking in, stir and simmer for 15 minutes.
5. Transfer to a serving dish and garnish with fresh coriander.

CHICK PEA AND POTATO CURRY

This is a very good dish to serve at a dinner party as it can be cooked in advance and re-heated just before serving. In fact, it tastes much better the day after when the chick peas have had time to absorb all the spices. Serve with fulecha for a buffet party or on a bed of plain boiled rice (pages 76 and 84) for a wholesome evening meal. You will need a pressure cooker for this recipe.

Cooking and preparation time: 20–30 minutes + overnight soaking

Serves: 6–8

225g (8 oz) chick peas
1 litre (2 pt) water
2 large potatoes (not peeled)
4 tbsp cooking oil
1 tsp mustard seeds
1 tsp cumin seeds
¼ tsp asafoetida powder
1 large onion, chopped
3 cloves garlic, peeled
2.5cm (1 in) root ginger, peeled
1½ tsp salt
1 tsp chilli powder
3 tbsp ground coriander
2 tsp ground turmeric
2 tsp sugar
1 tbsp sesame seeds
400g (14 oz) can tomatoes, chopped
juice of 1 lemon
2 tbsp green coriander, chopped

1. Soak the chick peas overnight. Wash and place in a pressure cooker with 1 litre (2 pts) of water and cook at high pressure for approximately 20 minutes, or until tender.
2. Meanwhile, boil the potatoes in a separate pan until just cooked. Remove from the water and allow to cool completely. Peel and cut into 2.5cm (1 in) cubes. (Leaving the skins on ensures they don't break up in cooking.)
3. Heat the oil in a large pan. When hot, add the mustard and cumin seeds, cover, and allow to 'pop' for a few seconds. Then add the asafoetida and quickly throw in the chopped onion. Stir, and cook,

covered, for 3 minutes, or until lightly browned. Stir occasionally.

4. Mince the garlic and ginger and add to the pan. Stir fry for approximately 30 seconds then add the salt, chilli powder, ground coriander, turmeric, sugar and sesame seeds. Stir fry for 1 minute and add the chopped tomatoes.

5. Bring to the boil and simmer for 5 minutes. Then add the cubed potatoes, cooked chick peas with 300ml (½ pt) of the cooking liquid and the lemon juice. Stir well, bring to the boil and simmer for 5 minutes.

6. If a thicker curry is wanted, boil rapidly with the lid off until the desired consistency is reached.

7. Serve garnished with chopped fresh coriander.

TARKA DHAL

The mixture of the three pulses gives this dish an unusual taste and texture. It should have a thick, porridge-like consistency. Serve it with puris and Mixed Vegetable Rice (pages 74 and 88). You will need a pressure cooker for this recipe.

Cooking and preparation time: 1 hour 10 minutes   *Serves:* 6–8

115g (4 oz) split mung beans
115g (4 oz) split chick peas
115g (4 oz) split pigeon peas
1 tbsp split black beans
1 litre (2 pts) boiling water
3 tbsp cooking oil
1 tsp mustard seeds
1 tsp cumin seeds
¼ tsp asafoetida powder
2 tbsp green coriander, chopped
2 tsp salt
1 tsp ground turmeric
1 tsp chilli powder
2 tbsp ground coriander

(continued overleaf)

225g (8 oz) can chopped tomatoes
2.5cm (1 in) root ginger, peeled and grated
2 tbsp jaggery or brown sugar
2 green chillies

1. Mix together the split mung beans, chick peas and pigeon peas and soak in warm water for 30 minutes. Soak the split black beans separately.
2. Wash the mixed pulses and place in a pressure cooker with 1 litre (2 pt) of boiling water. Pressure cook for 30 minutes at a low setting. The pulses should now be mushy.
3. Wash and drain the split black beans.
4. Heat the oil in a heavy bottomed pan. When hot, add the mustard and cumin seeds, cover and allow to 'pop' for a few seconds before adding the asafoetida and the split black beans, but take care as this will splatter. Reduce the heat, add the chopped green coriander and stir fry for 1 minute.
5. Now add the salt, turmeric, chilli powder and ground coriander and stir fry for another minute.
6. Stir in the chopped tomatoes and grated ginger. Bring to the boil and simmer for 5 minutes.
7. Add the jaggery or brown sugar.
8. Slit the chillies lengthwise and add to the tomato mixture, remembering to wash your hands thoroughly after handling them.
9. Lastly, add the cooked pulses mixture. Boil away until thick and soupy.

ORANGE CHANA DHAL

With its thick, orange flavoured sauce, this split chick pea curry dish makes a wonderful evening meal. It is also high in protein. Serve it with layered chapattis, plain boiled rice and some green salad or, for a dinner party, with other vegetable dishes.

Cooking and preparation time: 45–50 minutes   *Serves:* 4

225g (8 oz) split chick peas
500ml (1 pt) warm water
3 cloves garlic, peeled
3 green chillies
6 tbsp cooking oil
1 tsp mustard seeds
1 tsp cumin seeds
¼ tsp asafoetida powder
1 tsp ground turmeric
1½ tsp salt
500ml (1 pt) hot water
juice of 1 orange
2 tbsp green coriander, chopped for garnish

1. Soak the split chick peas in the warm water for 30 minutes. Wash them in several changes of water and drain.
2. Mince the garlic and chillies together and keep aside. (Don't forget to wash your hands after handling the chillies.)
3. Heat the oil in a heavy based pan. Add the mustard and cumin seeds and allow to 'pop' for a few seconds with the lid on.
4. Add the asafoetida and the drained chick peas and quickly cover the pan to prevent the oil from splattering. After about 10 seconds, uncover the pan and add the turmeric, salt and the minced garlic and chillies and mix well. Cook for 1 minute, stirring continuously, then add the hot water. Bring to the boil, cover and cook for 15 minutes or until the chick peas are tender. Stir occasionally during this time and add more hot water if required.
5. Lastly, stir in the orange juice and simmer for 1 minute. Empty into a serving dish and sprinkle with the chopped coriander.

WHITE CHANA DHAL

White chick pea curry is a traditional dish in the Punjab and northern parts of India. It is a very special dish for dinner parties, wedding parties and picnics. It is usually served with bhaturas, puris, chapattis, or even pitta bread. It also makes a good filling for toasted sandwiches.

Cooking and preparation time: 11 hours 40 minutes   *Serves:* 4

340g (12 oz) white chick peas
900ml (1½ pt) water for soaking chick peas
900ml (1½ pt) water for boiling chick peas
1 tsp salt
60ml (2 fl oz) cooking oil
½ tsp cumin seeds
½ tsp black mustard seeds
2 large onions, finely chopped
3 green chillies, finely chopped
2 tsp tomato purée
½ tsp chilli powder
1½ tsp tandoori masala
1 tsp turmeric powder
½ tsp garlic powder
1½ tsp garam masala
30ml (1 fl oz) lemon juice

For garnishing
small tomato, cut into rings
1 onion, cut into small rings
small amount green coriander, chopped

1. Wash the chick peas as described in the introduction.
2. Soak the chick peas overnight in the water.
3. Next day, drain the water. Place the chick peas in a large cooking pot, add the fresh water and the salt, and bring the mixture to the boil. Reduce the heat, cover the pan and simmer gently for about 1 hour.
4. In a separate pan, heat the oil to a high temperature. Add the cumin and mustard seeds; cook for a few seconds until they are slightly brown. Add the onions and green chillies, and cook until the onions are golden brown. Add the tomato purée, chilli powder,

tandoori masala, turmeric powder, garlic powder, garam masala and lemon juice. Stir continuously and cook for a further 2 minutes.
5. Drain the chick peas, but save the water. Add the drained chick peas to the spice mixture. Cook for a further 2 minutes, stirring continuously. Add the water which was drained from the chick peas, reduce the heat, cover the pan and simmer for about 5 minutes.
6. Place the cooked chick peas in a serving dish and garnish with the tomatoes, onion and coriander. Serve while hot, or allow to cool and use as a filling for toasted sandwiches.

BLACK CHANA DHAL

Black chick peas are more common in southern India than in the north, and taste somewhat like white chick peas. They are not usually served in restaurants, and therefore are worth trying at home.

Cooking and preparation time: 11 hours 20 minutes   *Serves:* 4

340g (12 oz) black chick peas
900ml (1½ pt) water for soaking the chick peas
900ml (1½ pt) water for boiling the chick peas
1 tsp salt
60ml (2 fl oz) cooking oil
½ tsp cumin seeds
¼ tsp asafoetida
½ tsp black mustard seeds
2 tsp tomato purée
½ tsp chilli powder
1 tsp tandoori powder
½ tsp turmeric powder
4 green chillies, finely chopped
1 tsp garam masala
30ml (1 fl oz) lemon juice
450ml (15 fl oz) water for cooking
small amount green coriander, chopped

(continued overleaf)

1. Wash the chick peas as described in the introduction.
2. Soak the chick peas overnight in the water.
3. Next day, drain the water. Add the fresh water and the salt and bring the mixture to the boil. Reduce the heat, cover the pan and simmer gently for about 1 hour.
4. Heat the oil to a high temperature, in a separate pan or wok. Add the cumin seeds, asafoetida, and the mustard seeds. Cook for a few seconds. Add the tomato purée, chilli powder, tandoori masala, turmeric powder, green chillies, garam masala and lemon juice. Stir well and cook for a further few seconds.
5. Now add the chick peas and the water for cooking. Bring the water to the boil; lower the heat and then simmer gently for a further 15 minutes.
6. Transfer the contents to a serving dish and garnish with fresh green coriander.

BLACK EYE BEAN DHAL

Black eye beans taste similar to chick peas, and are usually served with rice.

Note: the beans must be cooked for at least 20 minutes, otherwise they could cause indigestion.

Cooking and preparation time: 11 hours   *Serves:* 4

225g (8 oz) black eye beans
900ml (1½ pt) water for soaking
60ml (2 fl oz) cooking oil
½ tsp cumin seeds
½ tsp black mustard seeds
1 tsp salt
1 tsp turmeric powder
1 tsp chilli powder
1 tsp coriander powder
1 tsp cumin powder
2 tsp tomato purée
600ml (1 pt) water for cooking
small amount of fresh coriander, chopped

1. Soak the beans overnight in the water.
2. Wash the beans as described in the introduction.
3. Heat the oil to a high temperature, in a large pan. Add the cumin and mustard seeds and let it cook for a few seconds. Add the washed beans, salt, turmeric powder, chilli powder, coriander powder, cumin powder and tomato purée. Mix well and cook for about 2 minutes, stirring continuously.
4. Add the water, bring to the boil, lower the heat, cover the pan and simmer for about 25 minutes, stirring every 5–7 minutes.
5. Transfer the contents to a serving dish and garnish with the fresh coriander. Serve while hot.

CHANA AND MARROW DHAL

Split pulses are sometimes cooked mixed with vegetables. Marrow makes a very good addition to Chana Dhal and is well worth a try. For this recipe you need a pressure cooker.

Cooking and preparation time: 1 hour 20 minutes   *Serves:* 4

115g (4 oz) split chick peas or lentils
225g (8 oz) marrow, peeled and diced into small cubes
900ml (1½ pt) water
1 tsp salt
60ml (2 fl oz) cooking oil
115g (4 oz) onions, finely chopped
85g (3 oz) tomatoes, finely chopped
1 tsp turmeric powder
1 tsp chilli powder
1 tsp garam masala
3 green chillies, finely chopped
2 tsp lemon juice
small amount green coriander, chopped

1. Wash the pulses as described in the introduction.
2. Place the washed pulses and marrow in a pressure cooker. Add the water and salt, cover and cook for about 30 minutes on high

(continued overleaf)

pressure. Switch off the heat after this time but leave the pulses cooking in the pressure cooker for another 30 minutes.

3. Heat the oil to a high temperature, in another pan. Add the onions and cook them until they are golden brown. Add the tomatoes, turmeric powder, chilli powder, garam masala, green chillies and the lemon juice. Cook this spice mixture for about another 2 minutes.

4. Add the spice mixture to the pulses, stir well and cook together for about 5 minutes, stirring every 2–3 minutes.

5. Transfer the pulse mixture to a serving dish and garnish with the coriander. Serve hot.

SAMBHAR

This recipe is different in the way pulses and vegetables come together in one dish. It is normally served with Idli (page 47) or Masala Dhosa (page 44) but can also be served with rice. Reduce it by boiling to a thick soup-like consistency and serve in a gravy boat to pour over your Idli or Masala Dhosa as desired. This is originally a South Indian dish but is very popular all over India.

You will need a pressure cooker for this recipe.

Serves: 4–6

Cooking and preparation time: 2 hours 10–15 minutes

170g (6 oz) split pigeon peas
1500ml (3 pt) water
50g (2 oz) frozen peas
1 small potato, cubed
1 small carrot, cubed
1 small onion, sliced
1 small aubergine, chopped
4–5 florets of cauliflower
water for boiling
8 tbsp cooking oil
1 tsp mustard seeds
1 tsp cumin seeds

pinch asafoetida powder
2 tsp salt
1½ tsp ground turmeric
2.5cm (1 in) root ginger
3 cloves garlic
225g (8 oz) can tomatoes
2.5cm (1 in) cinnamon stick
4 cloves
3 tbsp ground coriander
1½ tsp chilli powder
small piece tamarind, soaked in boiling water
2 tbsp jaggery or brown sugar
juice of 1 lemon
5 curry leaves

1. Boil the pigeon peas for 1 hour in the water or pressure cook for 20 minutes at high pressure, whisk and allow to simmer. In another pan boil all the vegetables (except the canned tomatoes) in some water for 10 minutes and drain.

2. Heat 4 tbsp of the oil, add the mustard and cumin seeds, cover and allow to 'pop', then add a pinch of asafoetida powder and immediately add all the cooked vegetables. Add the salt and turmeric and mix well. Mince the ginger, garlic and tomatoes, and add to the vegetables. Simmer the vegetable mixture for 5 minutes and then add to the cooked pigeon peas.

3. Heat the remaining 4 tbsp of oil, add the cinnamon, cloves and ground coriander, and chilli powder and stir fry for 1 minute. Add to the pigeon peas and continue to simmer for another 10 minutes.

4. Strain all the juice out of the tamarind and add to the pulses with the jaggery, lemon juice and curry leaves. Taste and adjust seasoning. Simmer for another 30 minutes.

SPLIT PEA DHAL

Many people in India are essentially vegetarian. This dish of split pigeon pea soup, when served with plain boiled rice, a vegetable and a yoghurt dish, provides the protein in this typical vegetarian meal.

Cooking and preparation time: 1 hour 30 minutes   *Serves:* 6

125g (4 oz) split pigeon peas
1.5 litres (3 pt) boiling water
1 tsp fenugreek seeds
1 green chilli
2 tbsp jaggery or brown sugar
400g (14 oz) can of tomatoes
2.5cm (1 in) root ginger
2 tbsp oil
1 whole dry red chilli
1 tsp mustard seeds
1 tsp cumin seeds
1 pinch asafoetida powder
2 tsp salt
1½ tsp chilli powder
1 tsp ground turmeric
2 tbsp ground coriander
juice of 1 lemon
3 tbsp chopped green coriander for serving

1. Soak the split pigeon peas in a little boiling water for 10 minutes. Wash, drain and bring to the boil in a heavy based pan with 1.5 litres (3 pt) water and the fenugreek seeds. Cook for about 1 hour or until the split peas are cooked and mushy. Whisk thoroughly and continue to simmer gently.
2. Split the chillies lengthways and add to the pan with the jaggery or sugar. (Wash your hands thoroughly after handling the chillies.) Mince the tomatoes and root ginger.
3. In another pan heat the oil, add the whole dry red chilli, then add the mustard and cumin seeds, cover and allow to 'pop'. Remove from the heat and just before adding the tomatoes and root ginger, throw in a pinch of asafoetida powder. Bring to the boil, add the salt, chilli powder, turmeric and ground coriander and simmer for 5 minutes.
4. Add the tomato mixture to the pigeon peas and simmer for another 10 minutes. Add lemon juice and adjust seasoning as required. Sprinkle with chopped green coriander before serving.

DHAL DHOKRI

This split pigeon pea soup with dumplings is a delicious all-in-one dish. It can be served for lunch or for supper, on its own or accompanied with a salad. It is also a very good way of using up any left-over Dhal.

Cooking and preparation time: 40–45 minutes   *Serves:* 4
                     + 1 hour 20 minutes for cooking the Dhal

Follow the previous recipe for Split Pea Dhal, then make the Dhokri as follows:

2.5cm (1 in) cinnamon stick
5 cloves

Dhokri
115g (4 oz) gram flour
25g (1 oz) juwar flour (see page 283)
25g (1 oz) chapatti flour
½ tsp salt
½ tsp red chilli powder
1 clove garlic, crushed
0.5cm (¼ in) root ginger, finely chopped
¼ tsp ground turmeric
2 tsp ground coriander
pinch asafoetida powder
3 tbsp oil
water
oil and lemon juice to garnish

1. Bring the Dhal to the boil. Add the cinnamon stick and cloves and allow to simmer while you make the Dhokri.
2. Mix all the ingredients together and add enough water to make a stiff dough. Divide the dough into tangerine-sized balls and roll out one at a time on a floured board. Cut into diamond shapes and gently lower a few at a time into the bubbling Dhal. Allow the Dhal to reach boiling point between each addition of Dhokri. Simmer, uncovered, for 30 minutes.
3. To serve, dish out into individual soup plates, pour 2 tbsp of oil over it and a squeeze of lemon.

TOOVAR DHAL

This is one of the popular dishes of southern India, and has a sweet and sour taste. It is usually served with chapattis, bread, puris, parathas or rice. It is a dish which pleases vegetarians. For this recipe you need a pressure cooker.

Cooking and preparation time: 40 minutes *Serves:* 4

170g (6 oz) split pigeon peas
900ml (1½ pt) water
1 tsp salt
60ml (2 fl oz) cooking oil
½ tsp cumin seeds
½ tsp black mustard seeds
4 whole cloves
4 whole black peppercorns
¼ tsp asafoetida
1 tsp tomato purée
1 tsp turmeric powder
6 bay leaves
1 tsp chilli powder
2 green chillies, sliced into halves
½ tsp sugar
10g (½ oz) peanuts
15ml (½ fl oz) lemon juice
small amount green coriander, chopped

1. Wash the split pigeon peas as described in the introduction.
2. Place the washed pigeon peas in a pressure cooker, add the water and salt, and cook on high pressure for about 15 minutes after the initial boil whistle. Switch off the heat, but leave the pigeon peas cooking in the pressure cooker.
3. Heat the oil to a high temperature in a separate pan and add the cumin and mustard seeds, cloves, peppercorns, and asafoetida. Cook for a few seconds. Add the tomato purée, turmeric powder, bay leaves, chilli powder, green chillies, sugar, peanuts, and lemon juice. Stir continuously for a few seconds. Pour the boiled peas into the mixture and simmer gently together for a further 10 minutes, stirring every 2 minutes.
4. Transfer the peas mixture into a serving dish and garnish with the coriander. Serve hot.
5. The bay leaves and peppercorns are discarded and left on the plate while eating.

SPLIT MOONG DHAL

This is one of the many pulse curries usually served with chapattis, bread or rice. Like most pulse dishes it is popular with vegetarians.

Cooking and preparation time: 40 minutes   *Serves:* 4

170g (6 oz) skinless split mung beans
1 tsp salt
1 large onion, finely chopped
900ml (1½ pt) water
60ml (2 fl oz) cooking oil
½ tsp cumin seeds
½ tsp black mustard seeds
25g (1 oz) fresh garlic, peeled and finely chopped
85g (3 oz) plum tomatoes, peeled
1 tsp turmeric powder
1 tsp garam masala
1 tsp chilli powder
small amount green coriander, chopped

1. Wash the mung beans as described in the introduction.
2. Add the salt, chopped onion and the water to the washed mung beans. Boil the water, lower the heat and simmer gently for about 30 minutes, stirring every 5–7 minutes.
3. Heat the oil to a high temperature in a separate pan and add the cumin, black mustard and the chopped garlic. Cook for a few seconds. Add the tomatoes, turmeric powder, garam masala and chilli powder and cook for a further 3–4 minutes, stirring continuously.
4. Add this spice mixture to the boiled mung beans, and simmer gently for a further 5–7 minutes.
5. Transfer the mung bean mixture to a serving dish and garnish with the fresh green coriander.

WHOLE MOONG, DRY

This is one of the many pulse curries usually served with chapattis. It also makes a good filling for toasted sandwiches. It may also be served with rice and a meat curry dish.

Cooking and preparation time: 30 minutes   *Serves:* 4
                     + overnight soaking

170g (6 oz) whole mung beans
1200ml (2 pt) water for soaking mung beans
60ml (2 fl oz) cooking oil
½ tsp cumin seeds
½ tsp black mustard seeds
1 tsp turmeric powder
1 tsp garam masala
1 tsp chilli powder
2 tsp tomato purée
1 tsp salt
4 tsp soy sauce
450ml (15 fl oz) water for cooking
small amount green coriander, chopped

1. Soak the mung beans overnight in the water.
2. Wash the whole mung beans as described in the introduction.
3. Heat the oil to a high temperature, in a separate pan. Add the cumin and black mustard seeds, and leave it to cook for a few seconds. Add the washed mung beans, turmeric powder, garam masala, chilli powder, tomato purée, salt and soy sauce. Stir continuously and cook for about 3 minutes. Add the water and bring it to the boil.
4. Reduce the heat, cover the pan and simmer gently for about 30 minutes, stirring every 5–7 minutes.
5. Transfer the contents to a serving dish and garnish with fresh green coriander.

MOONG AND CHILLI DHAL

When cooked, this dish has a soft consistency rather like pâté. You could serve it for the first course at dinner parties with toast triangles or with toasted pitta bread bought from a supermarket. For best results, brush a little hot water on both sides of a pitta bread and toast under a hot grill until golden. Butter the hot pitta bread and cut into wide strips. Serve with the Moong and Chilli Dhal and a wedge of lemon. Alternatively, as a light main course or supper dish, serve with chapattis.

Cooking and preparation time: 30 minutes   *Serves:* 4–6

225g (8 oz) split mung beans
2 cloves garlic
2 green chillies
3 tbsp oil
1 tsp mustard seeds
1 tsp salt
1 tsp ground turmeric
750ml (1½ pt) boiling water
lemon wedges to serve

1. Wash and drain the split mung beans. Mince the garlic and chillies together. (Remember to wash your hands after handling the chillies.)
2. Heat the oil in a pan, add the mustard seeds and cover until they have stopped 'popping'. Add the split mung beans with the garlic and chillies. Stir fry for 1 minute, then add the salt and turmeric. Mix well.
3. Add the boiling water and simmer until most of the water has been absorbed. Test the mung beans between the thumb and forefinger. If more cooking is required, add a cupful of boiling water. Test again when the liquid has been absorbed.
4. Serve with wedges of lemon.

VALL DHAL

This is a dhal curry usually served with chapattis, bread, rice or pitta bread.

Cooking and preparation time: 2 hours 40 minutes   *Serves:* 4

225g (8 oz) split white beans
900ml (1½ pt) water
30ml (1 fl oz) cooking oil
½ tsp cumin seeds
½ tsp black mustard seeds
¼ tsp asafoetida
2 tsp tomato purée
1 tsp turmeric powder
1 tsp chilli powder
1 tsp garlic powder
1 tsp ginger powder
1 tsp salt
1 tsp garam masala
small amount green coriander, chopped

1. Wash the split white beans as described in the introduction. Then leave the beans to soak in the water for 2 hours.
2. Heat the oil to a high temperature, in a pan. Add the cumin seeds to the hot oil, and then a few seconds later add the black mustard seeds and asafoetida. Leave for a few more seconds and add the tomato purée, turmeric powder, chilli powder, garlic powder, ginger powder, salt and garam masala. Cook for a further 2 minutes, stirring continuously.
3. Drain the split beans, and save the water in which they were soaking, in another pan. Add the split beans to the spiced mixture. Cook for a further 2 minutes, stirring continuously.
4. Add the water in which the split beans were soaked to the above mixture. Bring to the boil and simmer gently for a further 30 minutes, stirring every 5 minutes.
5. Place the mixture in a serving dish and garnish with fresh coriander.

VALL KI DHAL

This dish of split white beans and yoghurt is very popular with the older generation as white beans have a slightly bitter taste. Because of this it is served with Kadhi (see page 56) which is tangy and so compensates for the bitter taste of the beans. This dish should have a thick porridge-like consistency. The carom seeds are used in this recipe to aid digestion as beans can be hard to digest.

You will need a pressure cooker for this recipe.

Cooking and preparation time: 50 minutes   *Serves:* 4–6

450g (1 lb) split white beans
1 litre (2 pt) boiling water
5 tbsp cooking oil
1 tsp carom seeds (see page 278)
1½ tsp salt
1 tsp ground turmeric
1 tsp granulated sugar
5 green chillies, chopped
2 cloves garlic, peeled
150ml (5 fl oz) natural yoghurt

1. Wash the split white beans and put in a pressure cooker with the water and cook for 30–40 minutes at medium pressure setting. For this recipe the beans should be very well cooked, almost mushy.
2. In another pan heat the oil and add the carom seeds. Very carefully add the beans with all the cooking water. Add the salt, turmeric, sugar, chillies and garlic and cook, stirring, for 5 minutes.
3. Add the yoghurt and blend well. Simmer with the lid off until the mixture is thick.
4. Place in a serving dish and serve hot.

WHOLE LENTIL DHAL

This is a rather mild dhal. It is usually served with boiled rice, chapattis or bread. Chilli powder can be used for making a hot dhal, otherwise paprika powder can be used for a milder taste. Fresh parsley or fresh green coriander can be used for garnishing.

Cooking and preparation time: 55 minutes   *Serves:* 4

170g (6 oz) whole lentils
900ml (1½ pt) water
1½ tsp salt
60ml (2 fl oz) cooking oil
½ tsp cumin seeds
1 large onion, finely chopped
2 tsp tomato purée
1 tsp turmeric powder
1 tsp chilli powder, or paprika powder for mild taste
2 tsp garam masala
1 tsp tandoori masala
some fresh parsley or fresh green coriander, finely chopped

1. Wash the whole lentils, as described in the introduction.
2. Place the washed lentils in the water, add the salt and bring to the boil.
3. Reduce the heat, cover the pan and simmer gently for about 45 minutes, stirring every 5–7 minutes.
4. Heat the oil to a high temperature, in a separate pan. When it is hot, add the cumin and the chopped onion. Cook together until the onion is golden brown. Add the tomato purée, turmeric powder, chilli powder (or paprika powder), garam masala and tandoori masala. Stir continuously and simmer the mixture for about 1 minute.
5. Add the spiced mixture to the cooked lentil dhal.
6. Simmer gently for about 3–5 minutes. Transfer the contents to a serving dish and garnish with the coriander or parsley.

SPLIT LENTIL DHAL

This dhal tastes very different from whole lentil and is usually served with plain boiled rice, or sometimes like soup, as a starter.

Cooking and preparation time: 40 minutes   *Serves:* 4

170g (6 oz) skinless split lentils
1200ml (2 pt) water
1 large onion, finely chopped
1 tsp salt
60ml (2 fl oz) cooking oil
½ tsp cumin seeds
½ tsp black mustard seeds
55g (2 oz) plum tomatoes, peeled
1 tsp turmeric powder
½ tsp garam masala
½ tsp chilli powder
small amount green coriander, chopped

1. Wash the split lentils as described in the introduction.
2. Place the split lentils, the water and the chopped onion in a large pan. Add the salt and stir well.
3. Bring the water to the boil, reduce the heat and simmer gently for about 30 minutes, stirring every 5–7 minutes. This boiled mixture can be served as soup if desired.
4. Heat the oil to a high temperature, in a separate pan or wok. Add the cumin and black mustard seeds and leave it to cook for a few seconds. Add the tomatoes, turmeric powder, garam masala, and chilli powder. Stir continuously and cook until the tomatoes have reduced to a pulp. This will usually take about 2–3 minutes.
5. Add the boiled lentil mixture to this spice mixture, reduce the heat and simmer gently for a further 5 minutes.
6. Transfer the contents to a serving dish and garnish with the fresh coriander. Serve hot.

VADDU

This dish has a special significance in the Hindu religion. Once a year women gather to pray for healthy babies and these prayer meetings always end with a communal meal of Vaddu and Rotla, an unleavened bread. At other times chapattis are served with this dish. (Rotla is regarded as poor men's bread and so it is not used in everyday cooking.)

You will need a pressure cooker for this recipe.

Cooking and preparation time: 2 days 15 minutes   *Serves:* 4–6

250g (8 oz) mung beans
115g (4 oz) whole lentils
warm water
5 tbsp cooking oil
1 tsp mustard seeds
1 tsp cumin seeds
4 green chillies, minced
2.5cm (1 in) root ginger, minced
2 cloves garlic, minced
2 tsp salt
1 tsp ground turmeric
500ml (1 pt) hot water

1. Combine the mung beans and lentils and soak overnight in warm water.
2. Drain and tie loosely in a warm, damp cloth and leave in a warm place for 2 days, but check twice a day to make sure the cloth does not dry out completely. By the end of 2 days the beans should have grown quite long roots.
3. Wash and drain the germinated vegetable mixture. In a pressure cooker, heat the oil and add the black mustard and cumin seeds and cover with the lid. Wait until they have stopped 'popping', then add the mung bean mixture and cook for a minute, stirring.
4. Reduce the heat, add the minced chillies, ginger and garlic. Also add the salt and turmeric and cook for a further minute. (Remember to wash your hands thoroughly after handling the chillies.)
5. Add the hot water, stir and close the lid of the pressure cooker and cook under low pressure for about 10 minutes. If a lot of liquid remains, reduce down by boiling rapidly with the lid off.

MORI DHAL

This simple pigeon pea dish is well worth trying. Spoon some on to a plate of plain boiled rice, add a dollop of ghee (page 246) and serve this with a bowl of hot Kadhi (page 56). It is quite delicious. It is also a very nutritious and economical meal which is very easy to make.

Cooking and preparation time: 30–40 minutes   *Serves:* 4

115g (4 oz) split pigeon peas
500ml (1 pt) boiling water
½ tsp salt
½ tsp ground turmeric

1. Soak the pigeon peas in 250ml (½ pt) of the boiling water. Leave to soak for 15–20 minutes. Wash the peas in several changes of water and drain.
2. Put the rest of the boiling water in a pan with the pigeon peas and bring back to the boil. Add the salt and the turmeric and simmer gently with the lid partly closed and cook for 15–20 minutes or until the mixture is soft and pulpy.
3. This dish should not be runny. If there seems to be too much liquid in the pan continue simmering with the lid off until a thick mushy mixture is left.

SPLIT MOONG AND SPLIT LENTIL DHAL

This is a mixed dhal, usually served with chapattis, bread, puris, parathas, rice or pitta bread. It can also be used like a soup, as a starter. It is very popular with vegetarians.

Cooking and preparation time: 45 minutes   *Serves:* 4

85g (3 oz) skinless, split mung beans
85g (3 oz) skinless, split lentils
900ml (1½ pt) water
1 large onion, finely chopped
1 tsp salt
60ml (2 fl oz) cooking oil
½ tsp cumin seeds
½ tsp black mustard seeds
2 tsp tomato purée
1 tsp turmeric powder
1 tsp garam masala
6 bay leaves
1 tsp chilli powder
small amount green coriander, chopped

1. Mix the split mung beans and lentils. Wash the pulses as described in the introduction.
2. Place the washed pulses, chopped onion and the water in a large pan and add the salt.
3. Bring the water to the boil, reduce the heat and simmer gently for about 30 minutes, stirring every 5–7 minutes.
4. Heat the oil to a high temperature, in a separate pan. Add the cumin and black mustard seeds and leave to cook for a few seconds. Add the tomato purée, turmeric powder, garam masala, bay leaves and chilli powder. Stir continuously and cook for a few seconds.
5. Pour the boiled pulses into the mixture, and simmer for a further 5 minutes.
6. Transfer the mixture to a serving dish and garnish with fresh coriander.
7. The bay leaves are discarded and left on the plate, while eating.

RED KIDNEY BEAN DHAL

This is a very popular curry all over India. It is usually served with chapattis, bread, pitta bread, puris, parathas, or simply rice. If you like sweet and sour dishes then sugar can be added to give it a slightly sweeter taste. This makes it very versatile. For this recipe you need a liquidiser.

Note: red kidney beans must be boiled for at least 1 hour as indicated in this recipe, otherwise they could be poisonous.

Cooking and preparation time: 2 hours 20 minutes   *Serves:* 4

170g (6 oz) red kidney beans
1200ml (2 pt) water
1 tsp salt
55g (2 oz) plum tomatoes, peeled
2 green chillies
25g (1 oz) fresh garlic, peeled
60ml (2 fl oz) cooking oil
½ tsp cumin seeds
½ tsp black mustard seeds
1 large onion, finely chopped
1 tsp tandoori masala
1 tsp turmeric powder
1 tsp garam masala
1 tsp sugar (optional)
30ml (1 fl oz) lemon juice
1 tsp tomato purée
½ tsp chilli powder
small amount green coriander, chopped

1. Boil the beans in the salted water for about 1 hour and 15 minutes. This will make the beans soft. (The test is whether you are able to pulp the bean easily, with your fingers.)
2. Place the tomatoes, green chillies, and garlic in a liquidiser, and blend to a thickish paste.
3. Heat the oil to a high temperature, in a large pan. Add the whole cumin and mustard seeds and cook for a few seconds. Add the onion and cook until it is golden brown.

(continued overleaf)

4. Add the contents of the liquidiser, tandoori masala, turmeric powder, garam masala, sugar (if required), lemon juice, tomato purée and chilli powder. Cook together for a further 1 minute.
5. Add the beans with the water. Lower the heat, and simmer gently for a further 30 minutes, stirring every 5–7 minutes.
6. Transfer the contents to a serving dish and garnish with fresh coriander. Serve hot.

KIDNEY BEAN SAK

A very healthy, delicious tasting dish. Serve as a main course with chapattis and rice.

Cooking and preparation time: 40 minutes   *Serves:* 4

2 tbsp oil
2.5cm (1 in) cinnamon stick
5 cloves
3 black peppercorns
1 medium sized onion, sliced
2 tsp garlic, crushed
1 tbsp tomato purée
150g (5 oz) tomatoes, peeled and chopped
2 tsp coriander powder
¼ tsp turmeric powder
½ tsp chilli powder (or to taste)
400g (14 oz) can kidney beans, drained
125–250ml (¼–½ pt) water
salt to taste
handful of coriander leaves, chopped, for garnish

1. Heat the oil and add the whole spices and onion, and fry until the onion is light golden brown.
2. Add the garlic and tomato purée and fry for 2 minutes.
3. Then add the rest of the ingredients (*except* for the coriander leaves), cover and simmer for 30 minutes.
4. Garnish with the chopped coriander leaves before serving.

WHOLE URAD AND RED KIDNEY BEAN DHAL

This is a rather mild curry. Like all dhal curries, it is usually served with boiled rice or chapattis but can be served with bread. If you like hot curries then green chillies should be used, but otherwise a green pepper can be used instead.

Note: the black beans and red kidney beans must be boiled as indicated in the recipe, otherwise the beans could be poisonous.

Cooking and preparation time: 2 hours 40 minutes   *Serves:* 4

85g (3 oz) whole black beans
25g (1 oz) red kidney beans
1800ml (3 pt) water
1 large onion, finely chopped
2 green chillies, finely chopped, or 1 green pepper,
  finely chopped
1 tsp salt
30ml (1 fl oz) cooking oil
½ tsp cumin seeds
2 tsp tomato purée
½ tsp turmeric powder
1 tsp chilli powder
1 tsp garam masala
some fresh green coriander, finely chopped

1. Mix the black beans and red kidney beans. Wash the beans as described in the introduction.
2. Place the washed, mixed pulses in the water.
3. Add the chopped onion, the chopped chillies (or green pepper), and the salt, and bring to the boil.
4. Reduce the heat, cover the pan and boil gently, stirring every 15 minutes until the consistency is like thin porridge. This should take about 2½ hours.
5. Heat the oil to a high temperature, in a separate pan. Add the cumin, tomato purée, turmeric powder, chilli powder, and garam masala. Stir continuously and simmer the mixture for about 1 minute. Add the mixture to the dhal and simmer the dhal gently for another 3–5 minutes.
6. Transfer the cooked mixture to a serving dish and garnish with the fresh coriander.

SPLIT URAD DHAL

This dhal curry is usually served with chapattis or bread. It can also be served with hot pitta bread. It is very popular with vegetarians. Green chillies can be used if you like hot curries, but otherwise a pepper can be used for a milder taste. For this recipe you need a liquidiser.

Cooking and preparation time: 1 hour 25 minutes   *Serves:* 4

170g (6 oz) skinless split black beans
1 large onion, finely chopped
1200ml (2 pt) water
1 tsp salt
85g (3 oz) plum tomatoes, peeled
3 green chillies or 1 green pepper, chopped
25g (1 oz) fresh garlic, peeled
25g (1 oz) fresh ginger, peeled
60ml (2 fl oz) cooking oil
½ tsp cumin seeds
½ tsp black mustard seeds
1 tsp turmeric powder
1 tsp chilli powder
1 tsp garam masala
small amount green coriander, chopped

1. Wash the black beans as described in the introduction.
2. Place the washed beans, chopped onion and the water in a large pan. Add the salt.
3. Bring the water to the boil, reduce the heat, and simmer gently for about 1 hour, stirring every 5–7 minutes.
4. Place the tomatoes, green chillies, garlic and ginger in a liquidiser and blend into a thickish paste.
5. Heat the oil to a high temperature, in a separate pan. Add the cumin and black mustard seeds and let it cook for a few seconds. Add the contents of the liquidiser, turmeric powder, chilli powder and garam masala. Stir continuously and cook for 2–3 minutes.
6. Add this spicy mixture to the boiled pulses, and boil for another 5 minutes.
7. Place the mixture in a serving dish and garnish with fresh coriander.

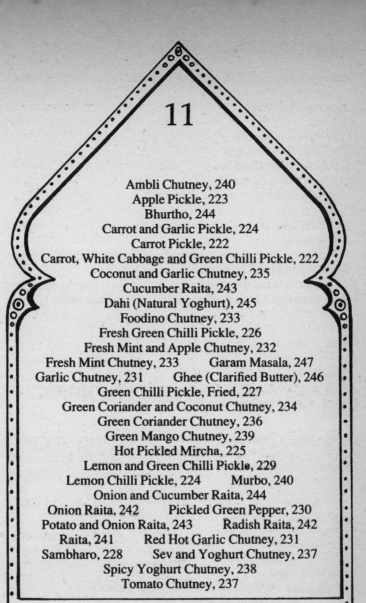

11

Accompaniments

CARROT PICKLE

Cooking and preparation time: 15 minutes   *Serves:* 4

225g (8 oz) carrots
1 tsp salt
½ tsp turmeric powder
30ml (1 fl oz) cooking oil
30ml (1 fl oz) lemon juice
2 tsp split mustard seeds
¼ tsp asafoetida

1. Peel the carrots; wash them and cut them into 2.5cm (1 in) long strips about 0.5cm (¼ in) thick.
2. Add all the above spices to the carrots, mix well, and transfer the contents to an airtight container.
3. This pickle can be stored for up to 2 weeks if kept in an airtight container and placed in the fridge. Use as and when needed.

CARROT, WHITE CABBAGE AND GREEN CHILLI PICKLE

Of the many Indian pickles served with main meals, this is one of the few prepared fresh, and served hot. Sugar can be added to give the pickle a slightly sweeter taste.

Cooking and preparation time: 30 minutes   *Serves:* 4

30ml (1 fl oz) cooking oil
¼ tsp cumin seeds
¼ tsp black mustard seeds
¼ tsp asafoetida
4 small green chillies, cut into halves lengthways
55g (2 oz) white cabbage, shredded
4 small carrots, cut into long, thin strips
1 tsp sugar (optional)
½ tsp salt

½ tsp turmeric powder
½ tsp tomato purée
90ml (3 fl oz) water
30ml (1 fl oz) lemon juice

1. Heat the oil to a high temperature, in a frying pan, and add the cumin, mustard seeds and asafoetida. Cook for a few seconds.
2. Add the chillies, cabbage, carrots, sugar (if used), salt, turmeric powder and tomato purée and cook for a further 2 minutes, stirring continuously. Add the water, and bring the mixture to the boil. Reduce the heat, and simmer gently until the water has evaporated. This will take about 15 minutes. Add the lemon juice and cook for a further 1 minute, stirring all the time.
3. Transfer the contents to a serving dish.

APPLE PICKLE

Cooking and preparation time: 15 minutes   *Serves:* 4

225g (8 oz) cooking apples
15ml (½ fl oz) cooking oil
1 tsp salt
¼ tsp garam masala
¼ tsp ground cumin
½ tsp split mustard seeds
¼ tsp asafoetida
15ml (½ fl oz) lemon juice

1. Peel the apples and cut them into about 1cm (½ in) cubes.
2. Heat the oil in a pan. Add the salt, garam masala, ground cumin, split mustard and asafoetida. Cook for a few seconds.
3. Switch off the heat, add the apples and lemon juice and mix well.
4. Transfer the contents to an airtight container.
5. This pickle can be stored for up to 1 week if kept in an airtight container and placed in the fridge. Use as and when needed.

CARROT AND GARLIC PICKLE

A very easy-to-make tasty pickle! Serve as an accompaniment with any of the main courses.

Preparation time: 2 hours 20 minutes   *Serves:* 4–6

3 large carrots
2 tsp crushed garlic
¼ tsp salt
1 tbsp oil
1 tsp tomato purée
½ tsp chilli powder
5 whole green chillies, sliced lengthwise (optional)

1. Peel the carrots and slice thinly, lengthways.
2. Mix with the rest of the ingredients and allow to marinate for at least 2 hours before serving.

Note: wash hands thoroughly after handling chillies.

LEMON CHILLI PICKLE

This, again, is easy to make but very tasty! Serve with whatever takes your fancy!

Preparation time: 20 minutes + 2 weeks for maturing
                                                Serves: several

2 lemons, sliced
10 green chillies, slit lengthwise
3 tbsp lemon juice
125ml (¼ pt) water
1 tsp turmeric powder
1 tbsp salt

1. Mix all the ingredients together in a glass bowl. Transfer into a glass jar and seal tight.

2. Stir at least once a day with a wooden spoon for two weeks.
3. After two weeks the lemons will have softened and the pickle is ready to serve.

Note: metal bowls and spoons will taint the flavour of this pickle, so be sure to use glass and wood, as recommended.
Wash hands thoroughly after handling the chillies.

HOT PICKLED MIRCHA

These pickled chillies are very hot. They are readily available at Indian grocery shops but you may like to make them from fresh chillies. The split mustard seeds can also be obtained from Indian grocery shops. For best results use only fresh chillies.

Preparation time: approx. 2½ hours   *Serves:* several

450g (1 lb) green chillies – the long and thin variety
1½ tbsp coarse salt
1 tbsp fenugreek seeds, crushed
115g (4 oz) split mustard seeds
1 tsp asafoetida powder
2 tsp ground turmeric
135ml (4½ fl oz) oil
1 tsp mustard seeds
juice of 8 fresh lemons

1. Wash and de-stalk the chillies, cut into 2.5cm (1 in) pieces and split in half lengthways. Mix the salt into the chillies and set aside for about 2 hours, or until some liquid is seen in the bottom of the bowl. (Remember to wash your hands thoroughly after handling the chillies.)
2. Roast and crush the fenugreek seeds. In a bowl, mix together the split mustard seeds, asafoetida powder, turmeric and the crushed fenugreek seeds. Add to the chillies.
3. Heat the oil in a small pan, add the mustard seeds and cover with

(continued overleaf)

the lid until the 'popping' stops. Pour over the chilli mixture immediately.

4. Heat the lemon juice up to boiling point and allow to cool completely. Pour over the chilli mixture and mix thoroughly.

5. Bottle in clean sterile bottles (wash and dry off in the oven for 10 minutes at 200°C (400°F), gas mark 6) and store. It will be ready to eat after 2 weeks.

FRESH GREEN CHILLI PICKLE

Cooking and preparation time: 10 minutes   *Serves:* 4

55g (2 oz) green chillies
1½ tsp salt
1½ tsp split black mustard seeds
½ tsp turmeric powder
1 tsp cooking oil
60ml (2 fl oz) lemon juice
¼ tsp asafoetida

1. Remove the stems and slice the chillies into halves lengthways. (Remember to wash your hands thoroughly after handling the chillies otherwise they leave a burning sensation on the hands.)
2. Mix well all the other ingredients together with the cut chillies in a large bowl, and then transfer the contents to an airtight container.
3. This pickle can be stored for up to 2 weeks if kept in an airtight container and placed in the fridge. Use as and when needed.

GREEN CHILLI PICKLE, FRIED

Sugar can be added to give the pickle a slightly sweeter taste.

Cooking and preparation time: 20 minutes   *Serves:* 4

55g (2 oz) green chillies
30ml (1 fl oz) cooking oil
¼ tsp cumin seeds
¼ tsp black mustard seeds
¼ tsp asafoetida
½ tsp salt
½ tsp turmeric powder
15ml (½ fl oz) lemon juice
½ tsp sugar (optional)
30ml (2 fl oz) water

1. Remove the stems and slice the chillies into halves lengthways. (Remember to wash your hands thoroughly after handling the chillies otherwise the chillies leave a burning sensation on the hands.)
2. Place the cooking oil in a frying pan. Heat the oil to a high temperature; add the cumin, black mustard seeds and asafoetida. Leave to cook for a few seconds until they are slightly brown. Add the chillies, salt, turmeric powder, lemon juice, sugar (if used) and water. Bring to the boil. Reduce the heat and simmer for about 5 minutes.
3. Place the cooked chillies in a serving dish.

SAMBHARO

A quick and easy but delicious pickle made with very simple ingredients. Can be served hot or cold as an accompaniment with a main meal or parathas.

Cooking and preparation time: 25 minutes   *Serves:* 4–6

2 tbsp oil
1 tsp black mustard seeds
3 cloves garlic, finely sliced
1 large carrot, cut into fine strips
5–10 green chillies, cut into strips
1 small unripe mango, cut into fine strips (optional)
¼ cabbage, finely sliced
¼ tsp turmeric powder
2–3 drops lemon juice
salt to taste
water

1. Heat the oil, add the mustard seeds and garlic.
2. When the mustard seeds start popping, add the rest of the ingredients, with just enough water, if required, to prevent the mixture burning. Stir together.
3. Cover and cook on low heat for 20 minutes, stirring frequently.

Note: make sure the heat is on low when adding mustard seeds, as they are likely to pop.
Wash hands thoroughly after handling chillies.

LEMON AND GREEN CHILLI PICKLE

This is a pickle in which lemon and fresh green chillies are allowed to marinate in their own juices for about 3–4 days. It is not spicy, but very hot.

Cooking and preparation time: 4 days   *Serves:* 4

55g (2 oz) green chillies
4 tsp salt for green chillies
2 fresh lemons
1 tsp salt for lemons

1. Remove the stems and cut open one side of the chillies along the length, so that the chillies still remain whole. (Remember to wash your hands thoroughly after handling the chillies otherwise they leave a burning sensation on the hands.)
2. With a teaspoon fill the chillies with salt. The 4 tsp salt should be enough to fill all the chillies.
3. Slice the lemons into quarters, but do not cut them right through. Leave about 0.5cm (¼ in) at the bottom where the lemon is not cut. Ensure that the lemon still remains in one piece.
4. Now share the 1 tsp salt between the two lemons.
5. Transfer both the lemons and the chillies to an airtight container and leave it in a cool place (not the fridge) for about 4 days. The salt will draw out the juices from the lemons and chillies and these will marinate in their own juices.
6. This pickle can be stored for up to 2 weeks if kept in an airtight container and placed in the fridge. Use as and when needed.

PICKLED GREEN PEPPER

This pickle is usually served with plain boiled rice and Kadhi (see pages 84 and 56). Include a vegetable dish of your choice and Mori Dhal (page 215). This will keep well in a refrigerator for up to 2 days.

Cooking and preparation time: 12–17 minutes   *Serves:* several

250g (8 oz) green peppers
8 tbsp cooking oil
1 tsp mustard seeds
¼ tsp asafoetida powder
½–1 tsp salt
1 tsp ground turmeric
2 tbsp ground coriander
½ tsp chilli powder
3 tbsp gram flour

1. Wash and cut the peppers into 2.5cm (1 in) squares. Heat the oil in a non-stick frying pan, add the mustard seeds and cover for a few seconds. Wait until the 'popping' has stopped then add the asafoetida powder to the oil and throw in the green peppers.
2. Reduce the heat to low, add the salt and turmeric and stir the contents of the frying pan. Cover and cook on low heat for 10 minutes, stirring occasionally. If the peppers start to stick to the bottom of the pan, add 2 tbsp of water. Continue cooking until the peppers are tender.
3. Add the ground coriander and chilli powder and mix well. Sprinkle the gram flour over the peppers and cook, covered, for 1 minute. Stir and cook, uncovered, for a further 2 minutes.
4. Remove from the heat and allow to cool. Refrigerate when cool and use within 2 days.

RED HOT GARLIC CHUTNEY

This chutney can be served with any Indian meal. It is extremely hot and only half a teaspoonful is placed on the side of the plate to be incorporated into the meal a little at a time. Serve it with mild or medium curries to give people a chance to choose the degree of hotness they desire.

Preparation time: 5–7 minutes   *Serves:* several

15 cloves garlic
2 tbsp chilli powder
½ tsp salt
1 tbsp oil

1. Peel and crush the garlic. Work the chilli powder into the garlic. Add the salt and oil and mix to a smooth paste.
2. Keeps well for several weeks in a refrigerator.

GARLIC CHUTNEY

Garlic chutneys are not usually served at meals but are used in cooking many curry dishes. Instead of blending garlic and ginger in a liquidiser, a spoonful of garlic chutney can be used instead. This saves having to peel garlic and ginger every time. You need a liquidiser to prepare this chutney.

                              Makes: about 450g (1 lb) of chutney
Preparation time: 40 minutes

60ml (2 fl oz) water
115g (4 oz) green chillies
170g (6 oz) fresh ginger, peeled
115g (4 oz) fresh garlic, peeled
1½ tsp salt
60ml (2 fl oz) lemon juice

1. Place all the ingredients in a liquidiser and blend together.
2. Transfer the contents into a jar, and store in the fridge. This chutney can be kept for up to 3 weeks.

FRESH MINT AND APPLE CHUTNEY

Chutneys are usually served with all main meals as a small side dish, like pickles. This is a hot chutney and is very good with most rice dishes. Sugar can be added to give it a slightly sweeter taste. A liquidiser or blender is needed to prepare this chutney.

Cooking and preparation time: 15 minutes   *Serves:* 4

55g (2 oz) mint leaves
115g (4 oz) cooking apples, finely chopped
55g (2 oz) onions, finely chopped
55g (2 oz) green chillies
¾ tsp salt
30ml (1 fl oz) water
½ tsp turmeric powder
½ tsp sugar (optional)

1. Place all the ingredients in a liquidiser and blend them into a smooth paste.
2. Transfer the contents into a small serving dish and place in the fridge for a couple of hours.
3. The chutney is ready to be served. Unused chutney can be left in the fridge, and served again. This chutney must be used within 7 days.

Note: in all recipes using chillies, wash hands thoroughly after handling them.

FRESH MINT CHUTNEY

This is a mild chutney, often served with main meals. Sugar can be added to give it a slightly sweeter taste. Either pomegranate seeds or lemon can be used. A liquidiser or blender is needed to prepare this chutney.

Cooking and preparation time: 15 minutes   *Serves:* 4

55g (2 oz) fresh mint leaves
1 small onion, finely chopped
½ tsp salt
½ tsp cumin seeds
½ tsp sugar (optional)
½ tsp pomegranate seeds or ½ tsp lemon juice
10g (½ oz) green chillies
30ml (1 fl oz) water

1. Place all the ingredients in a liquidiser and blend them into a smooth paste.
2. Transfer the contents to a serving dish.
3. Like all chutneys this can be stored in a cool place and served again. This chutney must be used in 3 to 4 days.

FOODINO CHUTNEY

This chutney made with fresh mint and chillies is excellent with bhajis.

Preparation time: 10 minutes   *Serves:* 4–6

handful of fresh mint leaves
5 green chillies
3 cloves of garlic, peeled
1 tbsp lemon juice
¼ tsp salt

1. Liquidise all the ingredients together and serve!

GREEN CORIANDER AND COCONUT CHUTNEY

This is another yoghurt dish to serve with curries or pulses. As it is quite hot serve it with a mild curry. It can also be served with bhajis or samosas (pages 40–41 and 31–34).

Preparation time: 5–7 minutes   *Serves:* several

1 bunch green coriander
½ fresh coconut
4 green chillies
1cm (½ in) root ginger
1 tsp cumin seeds
500ml (1 pt) natural yoghurt
1½ tsp salt

1. Wash and chop the coriander finely. Grate the coconut, mince the chillies and ginger together and coarsely grind the cumin seeds. (Wash hands thoroughly after handling the chillies.)
2. Combine all the ingredients together and mix thoroughly until quite smooth.
3. Keeps, refrigerated, for up to 1 week.

COCONUT AND GARLIC CHUTNEY

This chutney will keep well in a refrigerator for up to a week. Serve with any of the pulse dishes in this book. Use sparingly as this is quite a hot chutney. You will need a liquidiser.

Preparation time: 5–10 minutes   *Serves:* several

115g (4 oz) fresh coconut
115g (4 oz) garlic
2.5cm (1 in) root ginger
6 green chillies
½ tsp salt
juice of 1 lemon

1. Grate the coconut and peel the garlic. Chop up the ginger and chillies into small pieces. (Wash hands thoroughly after handling the chillies.)
2. Put all the ingredients in a liquidiser and liquidise until smooth, or grind together into a smooth paste.
3. Keeps, refrigerated, for up to 1 week.

GREEN CORIANDER CHUTNEY

The green coriander in this recipe should be rinsed in several changes of water to get rid of any soil still stuck to the leaves and stems. Serve it with Kadhi (page 56) and a vegetable or pulse dish. This is a hot chutney, so use it sparingly. Mix a little at a time into your food according to taste.

Preparation time: 5–7 minutes   *Serves:* several

1 bunch green coriander
6 green chillies
2 cloves garlic
2 tsp cumin seeds
½ tsp salt
juice of 1 lemon
1 tbsp oil

1. Mince the coriander, chillies and garlic. Crush the cumin seeds and add to the chilli mixture with the salt, lemon juice and oil. Mix thoroughly and use sparingly as it is very hot. (Remember to wash hands after handling the chillies.)
2. Keeps well, if refrigerated, for up to 1 week.

SEV AND YOGHURT CHUTNEY

Sev is a crispy spaghetti-like snack made from gram flour (ground chick peas). It is usually served sprinkled over another more substantial snack, such as Spicy Sweetcorn (page 46). There are shops which specialise in Indian snacks like Sev, but if you feel adventurous you could try making your own (see page 16). You will need a liquidiser for this recipe.

Preparation time: 3–5 minutes   *Serves:* several

500ml (1 pt) natural yoghurt
55g (2 oz) sev
3 green chillies
2 tsp cumin seeds
1½ tsp salt
½ bunch green coriander

1. Liquidise everything together. This is quick and easy and goes well with most curries.
2. Keeps, refrigerated, for up to 1 week.

TOMATO CHUTNEY

This chutney is served with a variety of snacks. Try it with bhajis or samosas. You will need a liquidiser for this recipe.

Cooking and preparation time: 10–12 minutes   *Serves:* several

2 large ripe tomatoes
1 large potato
2 tbsp ghee (see page 246)
1 tsp salt
4 green chillies
10–12 curry leaves – optional

1. Skin the tomatoes by putting them into hot water for 1 minute and then into cold water for 1 minute. The skins should then peel off with very little effort.

(continued overleaf)

2. Grate the potato and rinse in fresh water. Heat the ghee in a frying pan and cook the grated and drained potato until tender, stirring continuously. Allow to cool.

3. Add to the rest of the ingredients and liquidise. (Remember to wash hands after handling the chillies.) Bottle and store in the refrigerator. Can be kept for up to 1 week.

SPICY YOGHURT CHUTNEY

This is very quick and easy to put together and is ideal to serve with most curries. It is especially good served with Idli or Masala Dhosa (see pages 47 and 44). To make natural yoghurt at home see Dahi, page 245.

Preparation time: 5–10 minutes   *Serves:* several

500ml (1 pt) natural yoghurt
2 green chillies
1 bunch green coriander
2 cloves garlic
1½ tsp salt
2 tsp freshly ground cumin seeds

1. Put the yoghurt in a bowl and beat until smooth. Mince together the chillies, coriander and the garlic and add to the yoghurt. (Remember to wash your hands after handling the chillies.) Add the salt and freshly ground cumin seeds and mix well.

2. Taste and adjust the seasoning if necessary.

3. Keeps, refrigerated, for up to 1 week.

GREEN MANGO CHUTNEY

This delicious tangy chutney is ideal to serve with pulse dishes, plain boiled rice and a vegetable dish. It also goes well with Moong and Chilli Dhal or Orange Chana Dhal (pages 209 and 197). Green mangoes are seasonal and are only available in Britain during the spring and early summer months. You will find them at Indian grocery shops.

You will need a liquidiser for this recipe.

Preparation time: 5–10 minutes   *Serves:* several

225g (8 oz) green mango flesh, peeled
1 large onion, peeled
6 green chillies
2 cloves garlic
2 tsp cumin seeds
1 tsp salt

1. Roughly chop the peeled mango flesh and the peeled onion. Put the mango and the onion in the container of a liquidiser along with the rest of the ingredients. Liquidise until quite fine.
2. Empty into a glass bowl and adjust seasoning if required.
3. Will keep well in a refrigerator for up to 1 week.

AMBLI CHUTNEY

A very tasty chutney made with tamarind, delicious with most foods! Serve as a dip with bhajis, samosas or kebabs.

Cooking and preparation time: 15 minutes   *Serves:* 4

100g (3½ oz) dry tamarind
a few dates *or* 2 tsp sugar (optional)
1 tsp red chilli powder (optional)
500ml (1 pt) water
2 green chillies, finely chopped
coriander leaves, finely chopped for garnish

1. Boil all the ingredients (*except* the green chillies and coriander) in the water.
2. When the liquid has thickened and reduced in quantity, remove from the heat.
3. Strain through a sieve.
4. Add the green chillies and coriander and allow to cool.

MURBO

A delicious preserve, either eaten as a jam or as an accompaniment. Serve as an accompaniment with saks or with hot parathas for breakfast.

Cooking and preparation time: 1 hour   *Serves:* 6

450g (1 lb) unripe green mangoes
250ml (½ pt) water
300g (11 oz) sugar
5 cloves
5 cardamom pods, opened
5 black peppercorns
5cm (2 in) cinnamon stick

1. Peel the mango and slice or grate coarsely.

2. Boil the water, sugar and whole spices for 15 minutes.
3. Keep stirring until it forms into a syrup (if too thick, add more water).
4. Add the mangoes and allow to boil for at least 5 minutes.
5. Lower the heat, part cover and allow to simmer for 30 minutes, until the mangoes soften.
6. Remove from the heat and allow to cool before serving.

Note: this can be stored in a cool place for several weeks.

RAITA

A common yoghurt dish which is easy to make and very refreshing to eat. Serve as an accompaniment with any of the main meals or as a dip for bhajis, samosas or kebabs.

Preparation time: 15 minutes   *Serves:* 4

150g (5 oz) carton plain yoghurt
½ tsp cumin seeds, coarsely ground (optional)
¼ cucumber, coarsely grated
2 green chillies, finely chopped (optional)
½ handful of fresh mint, finely chopped *or* 2 tsp mint sauce
coriander leaves, finely chopped, for garnish

1. Mix all the ingredients (*except* the coriander) into a smooth paste.
2. Garnish with the coriander leaves before serving.

Note: wash hands thoroughly after handling chillies.

RADISH RAITA

This can be served as an accompaniment to vegetable dishes or as a dip at parties. Use crisps and savoury biscuits for dipping or try Fulecha to go with it (see page 76).

Preparation time: 3–5 minutes   *Serves:* several

55g (2 oz) radish
2 green chillies
2 tsp crushed cumin seeds
1½ tsp salt
1 tbsp chopped green coriander
500ml (1 pt) natural yoghurt

1. Grate the radishes, reserving one for garnish. Chop the chillies finely (and remember to wash your hands thoroughly after handling them).
2. Combine the grated radish, chopped chillies, crushed cumin seeds, salt and the chopped coriander in a bowl.
3. Add the yoghurt and mix until smooth. Empty into a glass serving bowl and decorate with slices of the reserved radish.
4. Keeps, refrigerated, for up to a week.

ONION RAITA

This is a perfect accompaniment to a hot curry as it helps to cool it down. Try serving it with Vegetable Curry or Green Bean Sak (pages 169 and 102).

Preparation time: 5–10 minutes   *Serves:* several

1 large onion (chopped)
500ml (1 pt) natural yoghurt
1½ tsp salt
2 tsp crushed cumin seeds
1 tsp powdered mustard

1. Mix all the ingredients thoroughly until smooth.
2. Keeps, refrigerated, for up to a week.

CUCUMBER RAITA

This goes especially well with vegetable dishes. It is also the usual accompaniment to Split Pea Dhal (page 204).

Preparation time: 5–7 minutes   *Serves:* several

1 cucumber
500ml (1 pt) natural yoghurt
1½ tsp salt
2 tsp crushed cumin seeds

1. Grate the cucumber and squeeze out most of the liquid.
2. Combine all the ingredients and mix thoroughly until smooth.
3. Keeps, refrigerated, for up to a week.

POTATO AND ONION RAITA

Like all raitas this is served as a side dish and is especially good in the summer.

Cooking and preparation time: 30 minutes   *Serves:* 4

340g (12 oz) boiled potatoes
1 large onion, finely chopped
1 green chilli, finely chopped
450ml (15 fl oz) natural yoghurt
90ml (3 fl oz) cold, fresh milk
½ tsp salt
½ tsp chilli powder
½ tsp black pepper

1. Cut the boiled potatoes into small pieces.
2. Place the potatoes, onion and green chilli into a serving dish. Add the yoghurt and milk, and mix well.
3. Place the raita in a fridge.
4. When you are ready to serve, remove the raita from the fridge and add the salt, chilli powder and black pepper. Mix well and serve.

ONION AND CUCUMBER RAITA

Serve as a side dish.

Cooking and preparation time: 15 minutes   *Serves:* 4

450ml (15 fl oz) natural yoghurt
90ml (3 fl oz) cold milk
115g (4 oz) cucumber, peeled and sliced
1 large onion, chopped into small pieces
½ tsp cumin seeds
½ tsp salt
½ tsp chilli powder
½ tsp ground black pepper

1. Combine the yoghurt and milk in a serving dish and mix well.
2. Add the sliced cucumber, onion and whole cumin seeds. Mix well.
3. Place the raita in the fridge.
4. When ready to serve, mix salt, chilli powder and ground black pepper into the raita.

BHURTHO

This dish is made with the flesh of an aubergine. It can be eaten as part of a main course, as a hot dip or with chapattis, Dhal Khichri (page 90) and plain yoghurt.

Cooking and preparation time: 1 hour   *Serves:* 4–6

1 large aubergine (*must be large*)
oil for brushing
2 tbsp oil
1 small onion, finely chopped
2 tsp garlic, crushed
2 green chillies, finely chopped
salt to taste
water, if required

1. Brush the aubergine's skin with oil and grill until the skin is nearly burnt and the flesh of the aubergine is soft.
2. Peel the skin off the aubergine and mash the flesh into a pulp.
3. Heat the oil in a saucepan, add the onion and garlic and stir.
4. When the onion has softened, add the rest of the ingredients (*except* the water) and stir.
5. Cover and simmer on low heat for at least 20 minutes and add drops of water if the mixture starts to stick to the pan (there is usually enough moisture in the aubergine pulp to aid the cooking process).
6. Stir frequently during cooking.

Note: wash hands thoroughly after handling chillies.

DAHI (NATURAL YOGHURT)

This natural yoghurt is the easiest thing in the world to make. The only requirement is a good, thick tea cosy, large enough to go over the container you are using to set the dahi in. Do give it a try. You will never buy your yoghurt from a supermarket again!

Cooking time: 1 hour + leave to stand overnight

1 litre (2 pt) milk, semi-skimmed or full fat
2 tbsp natural yoghurt

1. Bring the milk to the boil and simmer for 5 minutes. Pour the milk into the container you have decided to make the yoghurt in. Glass or enamel containers are best for this purpose. Allow to cool for 40–50 minutes, until tepid. To test the temperature, dip a clean finger in the milk. It should be just bearable. Now take 3 tbsp of the warm milk and stir into the yoghurt until smooth. Add this mixture to the warm milk and give it a good stir.
2. Cover the container and slip a tea cosy over it. Leave overnight and you should have some lovely firm yoghurt in the morning.
3. Refrigerate and use within 3 days. Remember to save 2 tbsp of yoghurt to use as culture to make your next lot.

GHEE (CLARIFIED BUTTER)

Clarified butter is simple to make but it is very important to watch it all the time. It can quite easily boil over so make sure you have a large pan. A heavy based pan is preferable as it allows more even distribution of heat. A quantity of butter is suggested, but you may wish to make more or less. It is entirely up to you.

Cooking time: 10 minutes

450g (1 lb) butter

1. Place the good quality butter in a large, heavy based pan. Heat the pan gently until all the butter has melted. Continue to simmer the melted butter until it is clear and glass-like. If it threatens to boil over take it off the heat immediately and stir continuously until the froth subsides. Put the pan back on low heat and continue to stir until the melted butter is clear.
2. When this stage is reached, take the pan off the heat and stand for 2 minutes. This will allow the residue to sink to the bottom of the pan. Now, very gently, strain into a glass or enamel container with a lid to separate the clear ghee from the residue. Take care not to disturb the sediment which must be discarded.
3. The ghee will become firm as it cools. Keep in a cool place and use as required. If made properly it should last for 2 months or more.

GARAM MASALA

This mixture of spices is available from most Indian grocery shops but here is a recipe for those of you who wish to make your own. Use this mixture very sparingly sprinkled over curries. You will need a coffee grinder for this recipe.

Cooking and preparation time: 40 minutes

225g (8 oz) coriander seeds
125g (4 oz) cumin seeds
125g (4 oz) cardamom seeds
55g (2 oz) cinnamon sticks
125g (4 oz) black peppercorns
55g (2 oz) cloves
1 tsp grated nutmeg

1. Preheat the oven to 150°C (300°F), gas mark 2, and roast the coriander and cumin seeds separately, stirring occasionally, for half an hour.
2. Allow to cool, then grind each ingredient separately until very fine. Mix thoroughly and pack in an air-tight container until needed.
3. Will store for up to a year if kept air-tight.

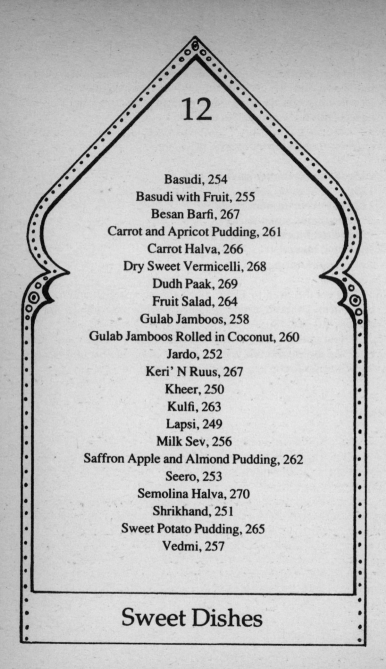

12

Sweet Dishes

LAPSI

A delicious, sweet starter made with cracked wheat. Like most Indian dishes, this is served along with the savoury dishes as the first course. The smell in the kitchen is quite amazing when Lapsi is being cooked. It is important to keep the Lapsi moving all the time while stir frying. This dish is cooked both on the hob and in the oven. Serve hot with poppadoms.

Cooking and preparation time: 1 hour   *Serves:* 6

55g (2 oz) butter
3 cardamom pods, opened
2.5cm (1 in) cinnamon stick
115g (4 oz) cracked wheat (bulgar)
25g (1 oz) sultanas
125ml (¼ pt) milk
125ml (¼ pt) water
½ tsp ground nutmeg
½ tsp ground cinnamon
55g (2 oz) sugar
55g (2 oz) desiccated coconut
2 strands saffron

For decoration
desiccated coconut

1. Melt the butter in a saucepan on low heat.
2. Add the whole spices and fry for 5 minutes.
3. Add the bulgar wheat, fry for 10–15 minutes, until golden brown, and keep stirring.
4. Add the sultanas and fry for a minute, until they swell.
5. Add the rest of the ingredients, keep stirring and bring to the boil.
6. Cover (or transfer to a lidded ovenproof dish, if necessary) and put in the oven at 180°C (350°F), gas mark 4, and cook for another 35–40 minutes, until it appears fluffy.
7. Sprinkle with desiccated coconut before serving.

KHEER

A sweet starter made with rice and spices. Serve hot with puris, parathas or chapattis.

Cooking and preparation time: 1 hour 20 minutes   *Serves:* 4–6
                                 + pre-soaking time

85g (3 oz) rice, washed and soaked for 30 minutes
55g (2 oz) butter
4 cardamom pods, opened
2.5cm (1 in) cinnamon stick
55g (2 oz) sultanas
500ml (1 pt) full fat milk
55g (2 oz) sugar
1 tsp ground cinnamon
1 tsp ground nutmeg
pinch of saffron
water, as required

1. Wash and soak the rice, then drain it.
2. Melt the butter and add the whole spices and sultanas and fry for at least 5 minutes.
3. Add the milk and the rest of the ingredients, *except* for the rice and water, and bring to the boil.
4. Add the rice and boil for a further 5 minutes.
5. Cover and simmer for 40 minutes, until the rice is mushy to touch. Add some water if the mixture begins to dry up.

Note: the consistency of this dish should be like rice pudding.

SHRIKHAND

This sweetened curd cheese is one of those sweet dishes that is served alongside savoury dishes as the first course of a meal. Serve puris (page 74) with this dish and sprinkle with the almonds, pistachios and cardamom seeds just before serving. Unused Shrikhand will keep in the refrigerator for up to a week.

Preparation time: 1 hour   *Serves:* 6

450g (1 lb) curd cheese
1 tbsp natural yoghurt
450g (1 lb) caster sugar
few strands saffron, soaked in 1 tbsp milk
115g (4 oz) almonds (blanched and sliced)
55g (2 oz) pistachios (chopped)
1 tsp ground cardamom seeds

1. Whisk the curd cheese, yoghurt and sugar together. Cover and leave for 1 hour for the sugar to dissolve. Whisk again, add the milk with the saffron in and mix well.
2. Place in the refrigerator and serve cold, sprinkled with the almonds, pistachios and cardamom seeds.

JARDO

This is a sweet rice dish made with exotic ingredients, for those with a very sweet tooth. Serve as a starter with poppadoms.

Cooking and preparation time: 50 minutes + pre-soaking time

Serves: 4

250g (9 oz) rice, washed and pre-soaked for 30 minutes
½ tsp yellow food colouring
250ml (½ pt) water
150g (5 oz) granulated sugar
¼ tsp cardamom seeds
pinch of saffron
150g (5 oz) pineapple chunks
25g (1 oz) chopped dates (optional)
55g (2 oz) butter
5cm (2 in) cinnamon stick
4 cardamom pods
25g (1 oz) sultanas

For decoration
55g (2 oz) almonds and pistachios, coarsely chopped
desiccated coconut

1. Wash and soak the rice, then drain and boil for 35 minutes in fresh water with half the colouring. Drain.
2. In another saucepan put the 250ml (½ pt) water, the sugar, cardamom seeds, saffron and the rest of the colour and boil until a syrup forms and the liquid has almost reduced to half its quantity. (Be careful not to splash yourself as melted sugar is *very* hot.)
3. Add the pineapple and dates.
4. Add the rice to the syrup and mix until all the syrup has been absorbed by the rice.
5. In a separate pan, melt the butter, add the cinnamon, cardamom pods and sultanas.
6. Add all this to the rice and leave in a switched off hot oven (at 200°C/400°F/gas mark 6) for 20 minutes.
7. Decorate with the nuts and coconut.

SEERO

Seero is made with semolina and spices. It heats up beautifully in a microwave oven or a conventional one. You can either serve it for the first course at a dinner party, along with vegetable and pulse dishes, or on its own at the end for dessert.

Cooking and preparation time: 1 hour   *Serves:* 4

85g (3 oz) butter
115g (4 oz) semolina
25g (1 oz) sultanas
1 tsp ground nutmeg
1 tsp ground cinnamon
55g (2 oz) sugar
125ml (¼ pt) milk
125ml (¼ pt) evaporated milk
2 strands saffron
water, as required

For decoration
handful of almonds, coarsely ground
desiccated coconut

1. Melt the butter on low heat, add the semolina and fry for 20 minutes, stirring frequently.
2. Add the sultanas and fry for 5 minutes, until they swell.
3. Add the rest of the ingredients (except the water) and bring to the boil, stirring vigorously all the time.
4. Cover and simmer for 30 minutes and keep stirring frequently. If the mixture begins to dry up before the semolina has cooked add drops of water as required.
5. When the semolina has cooked, i.e. almost doubled in quantity, it is ready.
6. Before serving, sprinkle with nuts and desiccated coconut. Serve hot.

BASUDI

This milk pudding is served with puris (page 74) as the first course of a meal with a vegetable dish as an accompaniment. It is served in small quantities as it can be very filling, and as a general rule it is served only at special occasions and dinner parties. It is a good idea to use a large heavy based pan for this to prevent the milk boiling over. Stir often and on no account leave it for any length of time. It can easily burn and stick to the bottom of the pan.

Cooking and preparation time: 1½ hours   *Serves:* 4–6

1 litre (2 pt) full fat milk
4 tbsp granulated sugar
1 tsp ground cardamom seeds
1 tbsp almonds, peeled and sliced
1 tbsp pistachios, sliced

1. Bring the milk to the boil and simmer, stirring occasionally, until thick and creamy. You should end up with approximately 375ml (¾ pt) of thickened milk.
2. Remove from the heat, add the sugar, ground cardamom seeds, sliced almonds and pistachios and stir until the sugar has dissolved. Allow to cool, stirring occasionally to avoid a skin forming on the surface.
3. Empty into a serving dish and refrigerate until required.

BASUDI WITH FRUIT

This milk pudding with fruit is a much lighter sweet dish and it is served either as part of the first course or on its own for dessert. It is an attractive looking dish and may be served quite successfully at a dinner party. It is important to stir often while it is cooling to avoid skin forming on the surface.

Cooking and preparation time: 25 minutes   *Serves:* 6–8

½ tbsp custard powder
1 litre (2 pt) full fat milk
6 tbsp granulated sugar
1 tsp ground cardamom seeds
2 tbsp almonds, peeled and sliced
425g (15 oz) can mixed fruit

1. Mix the custard powder with a little of the milk in a small bowl and keep to one side. Bring the rest of the milk to the boil and simmer for 15 minutes.
2. Add the custard powder paste, stir and remove from heat. Now add the sugar, cardamom seeds and almonds and allow to cool completely, stirring occasionally to avoid a skin forming on the surface.
3. When quite cold, strain the liquid out of the mixed fruit and add the fruit to the pan. Stir and empty into a serving dish and keep refrigerated until ready to serve.

MILK SEV

A sweet milk 'pud' made with vermicelli and spices which can be served hot as a dessert on its own, or as a starter, especially delicious with bhajis.

Cooking and preparation time: 1 hour   *Serves:* 4–6

115g (4 oz) butter
4 cardamom pods, opened
2.5cm (1 in) cinnamon stick
150g (5 oz) vermicelli
115g (4 oz) sultanas
1 tsp ground nutmeg
1 tsp ground cinnamon
750ml (1½ pt) milk
2 strands saffron
55g (2 oz) coarsely chopped almonds
55g (2 oz) coarsely chopped pistachios

1. Melt the butter on a low heat, add the whole spices and fry for 5 minutes.
2. Scrunch the vermicelli and add to the butter. Fry for 10 minutes until golden brown, stirring constantly.
3. Add the sultanas and fry for 5 minutes, still stirring frequently.
4. Add the rest of the ingredients and bring to the boil.
5. Cover and simmer for 40 minutes, until the vermicelli is tender to touch.

VEDMI

Even though these sweet stuffed chapattis are more time-consuming than many of the other sweet dishes they are well worth the time and trouble. If you do not have a microwave oven, put the cooked, drained pigeon peas in a large deep pan with the sugar and cook, stirring all the time until thickened. Take care when you do this as the mixture in the pan is very hot and will tend to splutter as it thickens. You will need a pressure cooker for this recipe.

Cooking and preparation time: 1 hour 20–30 minutes *Serves:* 4–6

225g (8 oz) split pigeon peas
1 litre (2 pt) hot water
225g (8 oz) granulated sugar
1 tsp ground cardamom seeds
½ tsp grated nutmeg
½ tsp cloves, ground
450g (1 lb) chapatti flour (ground wheat)
1 tbsp cooking oil
hot water
oil for shallow frying
melted ghee for serving

1. Wash the split pigeon peas and soak in hot water for 30 minutes. Strain and place in a pressure cooker with hot water to cover the peas by about 2.5cm (1 in). Pressure cook for 15–20 minutes at medium pressure. Remove from the heat and leave for 30 minutes before opening the pressure cooker. The pea dhal should be soft and pulpy. If it is still hard, cook for a few more minutes.

2. When cooked do not stir but drain off as much water as possible and then empty into a large glass bowl. Add the sugar and mix well. Cover the bowl with a plate and cook in the microwave oven at full power for 5 minutes. It should end up with a dry, dough-like consistency. If it is still too wet, give it more time in the microwave until the right consistency is reached. Allow to cool completely.

3. Mix in the cardamom, nutmeg and cloves. Form into large walnut-sized balls.

4. In another bowl, take the chapatti flour and make a hole in the middle. Put in the oil and gradually add enough hot water to form a soft dough.

(continued overleaf)

257

5. Make slightly smaller balls from this dough. Roll out each ball into approximately 5cm (2 in) circles. Place a ball of pea dhal in the centre and bring up the sides of the dough and press together at the top enclosing the ball of pea dhal completely. Gently flatten between the palms and dip in some flour. Roll out very carefully to a thick round shape about 7–10cm (3–4 in) in diameter.

6. Heat a tavi or frying pan over gentle heat. Place the Vedmi on the tavi or frying pan and cook on both sides for approximately 1 minute each side. (Very gentle handling will be necessary at this stage.) Lastly, trickle a teaspoon of oil around the Vedmi and cook for another 30 seconds each side. Serve hot.

7. It is much easier to cook all the Vedmi dry on the tavi first and then cook again with a little oil only when required. Pour over a tablespoon of melted ghee just before serving.

GULAB JAMBOOS

This is a very sweet dish, often served as a dessert after a hot curry. It can also be served at parties or with high tea. It may be served hot or cold depending on personal preference. For this recipe you need a deep frying pan or wok.

For the recipe to succeed make sure the syrup is right before you start frying your little balls of dough. When testing the syrup, allow to cool a little before touching it with your fingers as hot sugar will burn.

Serve these for dessert with a little of the syrup or with some ready made vanilla ice cream. Keeps well in a refrigerator for up to a week.

Cooking and preparation time: 30–45 minutes   *Serves:* 8–10

Syrup
425ml (15 fl oz) water
350g (12 oz) granulated sugar

Dough

225g (8 oz) powdered milk
55g (2 oz) plain flour
¼ tsp bicarbonate of soda
1 tsp ground cardamom seeds
1 tsp ghee, melted
milk at room temperature

oil for frying, approximately 1500ml (3 pt)

1. To make the sugar syrup, combine the water and sugar in a pan and bring to the boil slowly. Increase the heat and boil rapidly for 5 minutes. Test if the syrup is the right consistency by taking a teaspoon of the syrup, allowing it to cool and then, taking it between thumb and forefinger, pulling it to see if a 'string' forms. If the syrup is not ready, continue to boil and test at minute intervals. When ready, remove from the heat but keep warm.

2. Sieve the powdered milk, flour and bicarbonate of soda several times to incorporate air. Add the cardamom seeds and rub in the ghee very lightly. It is essential to be light with your fingers. Use enough milk to bind the mixture into a soft ball. Do not knead.

3. Still being very gentle, divide into grape-sized balls and fry in medium hot oil until golden.

4. Drain and throw straight into the hot syrup.

5. When all the Gulab Jamboos are in the syrup, allow to cool completely. Empty into a glass bowl and refrigerate.

GULAB JAMBOOS ROLLED IN COCONUT

When mixing the ingredients together, do it very gently with a fork. Finally go in with your hands and very gently form little sausage shapes just before frying. These are ideal to serve at dinner parties as they can be made 2 or 3 days in advance. They are good served with a scoop of ready-made vanilla ice-cream. You will need a deep wok or frying pan for this recipe.

Cooking and preparation time: 30–40 minutes   *Serves:* 8–10

Syrup
350g (12 oz) granulated sugar
280ml (10 fl oz) water

Dough
380g (13¼ oz) can unsweetened condensed milk
200g (7 oz) plain flour
55g (2 oz) semolina
3 tsp baking powder
150ml (5 fl oz) ghee
150ml (5 fl oz) natural yoghurt
4 tsp rose water
2 tbsp chopped almonds
1 tsp ground cardamom seeds
1 tbsp chopped pistachios
a few strands saffron
55g (2 oz) desiccated coconut
oil for frying, approx 1500ml (3 pt)

1. Make the syrup as in Gulab Jamboos (previous recipe) but the consistency must be thicker, similar to that of honey.
2. Combine all the other ingredients except the desiccated coconut. Shape the Jamboos into sausage shapes and deep fry until golden brown.
3. Soak in the hot syrup for a few minutes, drain and roll in the coconut.
4. Cool completely then put in the fridge.

CARROT AND APRICOT PUDDING

An excellent combination of flavours – must be tried! Serve scoops in a shallow fruit bowl.

Cooking and preparation time: 1 hour + setting time   *Serves:* 6

50g (2 oz) dried apricots
½ tbsp custard powder
375ml (¾ pt) milk
dash of rum, cognac or sherry (optional)
600g (1 lb 4 oz) carrots, finely grated
25g (1 oz) cashew nuts, chopped into small pieces
25g (1 oz) pistachio nuts, chopped into small pieces
150g (5 oz) sweetened condensed milk
115g (4 oz) evaporated milk

For decoration
240ml (8 fl oz) carton double cream, whipped
grated chocolate or desiccated coconut
almonds, coarsely chopped
cherries or kiwi fruit slices

1. Soak the apricots until soft (about 10 minutes) and cut into small pieces.
2. Mix the custard powder into a smooth paste with a small amount of milk.
3. Boil the rest of the milk (adding the alcohol, if using).
4. Add the carrots, stir and allow to cook for 5 minutes.
5. Stir in the cashew and pistachio nuts along with the custard paste, followed by the condensed and evaporated milks. Mix well.
6. Pour into a bowl and when cool put into the fridge to set.
7. Spread the double cream over and decorate.

SAFFRON APPLE AND ALMOND PUDDING

If you like apples then this dish is worth a try. It can be served with hot or cold custard, or cream.

Cooking and preparation time: 20 minutes   *Serves:* 4

450g (1 lb) eating apples
120ml (4 fl oz) water
115g (4 oz) sugar
a pinch of saffron
2 tsp cornflour mixed with 2 tsp water
115g (4 oz) almonds, finely chopped

1. Peel the apples and remove the cores. Cut the apples into chip-shaped pieces.
2. Mix the apples, water, sugar and saffron in a pan and bring to the boil. Lower the heat, cover the pan and let the apples simmer for about 5 minutes.
3. Add the cornflour mixed with the water, mix well and let the mixture simmer for a further 2–3 minutes.
4. Transfer the contents to a serving dish and garnish with the almonds. Serve hot or cold (depending on taste) with cream or custard.

KULFI

Kulfi is the Indian version of rich ice-cream, fit for a king! So, if you are up to it, have a try! It is very sweet and like most Indian desserts very heavy in calories. Most Indian children love kulfi. Serve decorated with cherries, ground almonds or chocolate sauce.

Cooking and preparation time: 40 minutes + freezing time

Serves: 6

2 medium sized eggs
200g (7 oz) sugar (or to taste)
200g (7 oz) evaporated milk
½ tsp ground cardamom seeds
½ tsp ground nutmeg
½ tsp vanilla essence
2 strands saffron (optional)
55g (2 oz) coarsely chopped almonds
55g (2 oz) coarsely chopped pistachios
250ml (½ pt) double cream, whipped

1. Separate the egg yolks from the whites.
2. Whisk the sugar, milk, cardamom seeds and nutmeg until frothy.
3. Add the vanilla essence and saffron, if using, to the egg yolks, beat and add to the milk mixture.
4. Whisk the egg whites until firm and add to the mixture.
5. Add the nuts and cream and mix very gently.
6. Freeze for ½–1 hour.
7. Remove from freezer, stir and place into moulds and re-freeze for 1–2 hours.
8. Allow to thaw for 10 minutes before serving.

FRUIT SALAD

This is an absolutely delicious fruit salad, right for any occasion! Serve plain or with ice-cream or single cream.

Preparation time: 40 minutes + chilling time   *Serves:* 6

150g (5 oz) mixed tropical fruit in fruit juice (ready bought)
2 passion fruits, halve, scoop out flesh and discard skin
1 pomegranate, peel and use *only* the seeds (flesh is bitter)
1 banana, sliced
1 hard pear, peeled and cubed
handful of seedless grapes, halved
2 kiwi fruits, peeled and sliced
1 small red apple, cubed
½ ripe mango, peeled and cubed
½ pawpaw, peeled, seeded and cut into chunks
6 lychees, peeled and seeded
½ star fruit, thinly sliced
2 tbsp sugar (optional)
1 tbsp alcohol of your choice (optional)

1. Mix all the ingredients together and chill for at least 1 hour before serving.

SWEET POTATO PUDDING

This is made with sweet potatoes and milk. This pudding is especially nice eaten cold on a hot summer's day. It will follow nicely after any of the main courses in this book.

Cooking and preparation time: 40 minutes   *Serves:* 4–6
                              + 2 hours chilling time

2–3 sweet potatoes, *not* peeled
water for cooking potatoes
375ml (¾ pt) milk
210ml (7 oz) carton single cream (optional)
sugar to taste
coarsely ground almonds for garnish

1. Place the sweet potatoes in boiling water, cover partly and cook on medium heat for 30 minutes, until the potatoes are easily squashed.
2. Peel the skin off the potatoes and mash into a purée.
3. Mix the potato purée with the milk and cream (if using), and sugar to taste.
4. Chill for at least 2 hours before serving, garnished with the nuts.

CARROT HALVA

This is a sweet and tasty carrot dish. It can be served hot or cold and this makes it more flexible.

Cooking and preparation time: 2 hours 40 minutes   *Serves:* 4

340g (12 oz) carrots
90ml (3 fl oz) water
¼ tsp ground cardamom or 3 whole cardamoms, crushed
a pinch of saffron
180ml (6 fl oz) milk
55g (2 oz) sugar
1 tsp melted unsalted butter or ghee
25g (1 oz) almonds (skinless)

1. Peel, and then grate the carrots.
2. Mix the grated carrots, water, cardamom and saffron in a large pan. Bring the water to the boil and then lower the heat. Cover the pan, and simmer gently for about 1 hour, stirring every 10–15 minutes.
3. Add the milk and sugar and simmer for a further 1 hour on a low heat.
4. Add the butter or ghee, and evaporate the milk on a gentle heat. This usually takes about 15 minutes, and at the end you are left with very little liquid in the carrots.
5. Transfer the contents to a serving dish and decorate with the almonds. Serve either hot or cold.

KERI' N RUUSS

Mango pulp flavoured with ginger, eaten as a cold soup. Serve chilled.

Preparation time: 2 minutes + 1 hour chilling time   *Serves:* 6

1 tbsp ginger powder
210ml (7 oz) carton single cream
450g (1 lb) tin mango pulp
2 tbsp granulated sugar

1. Mix the ginger with a little of the cream into a paste and then mix with all the ingredients (including the remaining cream), stir and chill for at least 1 hour before serving.

BESAN BARFI

This gram flour fudge dessert dish is not as sweet as gulab jamboos and is served cold. It tastes very much like fudge and can be stored for up to 1 week after cooking. It can also be served at high teas or picnics. For this recipe you need a deep frying pan or wok.

Cooking and preparation time: 4 hours 40 minutes   *Serves:* 4

110g (4 oz) sugar
120ml (4 fl oz) water
225g (8 oz) gram flour
115g (4 oz) ghee
115g (4 oz) gulab jamboo powder or milk powder
5 drops yellow food colouring or
   a pinch of yellow food colouring powder
¼ tsp ground nutmeg
¼ tsp ground cardamom
25g (1 oz) almonds, finely chopped

1. Place the sugar and water in a pan and bring the mixture to the boil. Simmer gently for about 8–9 minutes.

(continued overleaf)

2. Sieve the gram flour into a wok or deep frying pan and add the ghee. Cook the mixture on a very low heat, stirring continuously, until the flour is golden brown.

3. Add the gulab jamboo powder (or milk powder) and cook for another 2 minutes, stirring continuously.

4. Now add the sugar syrup. Stir continuously over a very low heat until the mixture is thick and sticky, very much like jam.

5. Remove the mixture from the heat, add the colouring, nutmeg and cardamom powder and mix well. Place the mixture in a greased tray. Garnish with almonds and leave it to cool down. While the mixture is still warm, cut it completely through, into cubes like fudge. Leave it to set for a further 4 hours. Separate the cubes.

6. This dessert is served cold.

DRY SWEET VERMICELLI

This is a sweet dish served as a dessert. It is not served in restaurants and therefore well worth trying at home.

Cooking and preparation time: 40 minutes   *Serves:* 4

85g (3 oz) sugar
450ml (15 fl oz) water
170g (6 oz) vermicelli
55g (2 oz) ghee
½ tsp ground cardamom
½ tsp grated nutmeg
25g (1 oz) almonds, finely chopped

1. Mix the sugar and water and bring the mixture to the boil.

2. Cook the vermicelli and ghee together, on a very low heat, stirring continuously, until the vermicelli turns golden brown. This usually takes 15–20 minutes.

3. Add the sugar syrup, cardamom and nutmeg and stir well. Bring the mixture to the boil, reduce the heat and simmer gently until the water has evaporated. This will usually take about 15 minutes.

4. Transfer the contents to a serving dish and garnish with almonds. Serve while hot.

DUDH PAAK

This is a sweet dish, similar to the traditional English rice pudding but with a difference. It is well worth trying. The rice soaks up the milk as it cooks and becomes plump while the milk thickens. It all ends up in a thick creamy pudding which is flavoured with exotic spices. It is usually served as a dessert and can be served hot or cold depending on choice.

Cooking and preparation time: 45–55 minutes   *Serves:* 4–6

75g (2½ oz) long grain rice
1 litre (2 pt) full fat milk
1 tsp ghee (page 246)
4 tbsp granulated sugar
1 tsp ground cardamom
1 tbsp almonds, peeled and sliced
1 tbsp pistachios, sliced
½ tsp grated nutmeg
almonds and pistachios, ground, for garnish
ground cardamom and nutmeg, for garnish

1. Wash the rice and soak for 5 minutes. Bring the milk to the boil in a large heavy based pan. When boiling, add the strained rice and the ghee and bring back to the boil.
2. Reduce the heat and simmer, stirring occasionally, until the mixture is quite thick. It should have reduced to half the original quantity. Remove from heat.
3. Now add the sugar, ground cardamom, sliced almonds, sliced pistachios and grated nutmeg.
4. Cool completely, stirring often to avoid skin forming on the surface of the pudding.
5. Pour into a serving dish and refrigerate for a few hours before serving.
6. Garnish with ground cardamom, nutmeg, chopped almonds and pistachios.

SEMOLINA HALVA

Semolina halva is usually served in Sikh and Hindu temples. It is popular with vegetarians. It is a very sweet dessert and contains a large amount of fat.

Cooking and preparation time: 45 minutes   *Serves:* 4

420ml (14 fl oz) water
115g (4 oz) sugar
¼ tsp ground cardamom
150g (5 oz) butter
115g (4 oz) semolina

1. Mix the water, sugar and cardamom and bring the mixture to the boil. Switch off heat.
2. In a large saucepan melt the butter. Lower the heat, and add the semolina. Stir continuously and cook until the semolina turns golden brown. This will usually take about 9–10 minutes.
3. Now add the water and sugar mixture, stirring continuously. Do this carefully, because, when first poured, the water will froth and may spit out of the pot. Make sure that you stir continuously, otherwise the mixture will become lumpy.
4. Increase the heat and bring the mixture to the boil. Lower the heat and cook for about a further 4 minutes, stirring continuously. The mixture will be a very thick paste.
5. Transfer the contents to a serving bowl and serve hot.

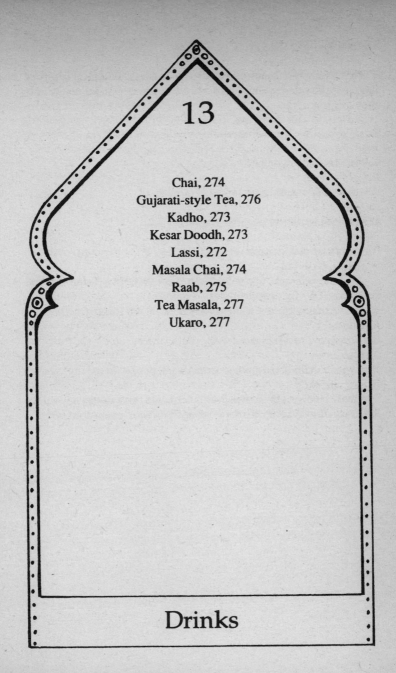

13

Drinks

LASSI

This is a yoghurt drink often served at meals. It may be served sweet or salty depending on personal preference and is especially nice as an accompaniment with the dry vegetable saks. It is supposed to cool the blood and in India it is given to farm workers for this reason. It keeps for up to three days in a refrigerator and you may like to have a jugful in the fridge during the summer months.

For this recipe you need a whisk.

Cooking and preparation time: 35 minutes   *Serves:* 4

250ml (8 fl oz) fresh natural yoghurt
300ml (½ pt) water
½ tsp salt or 1 tsp sugar

1. Mix the yoghurt, water and salt (or sugar) in a large jug and whisk together for approximately 5 minutes.
2. Leave the mixture (called lassi) to cool in the fridge for about 30 minutes.
3. Serve cold in tall glasses with a cube of ice.

Variations: Add ¼ teaspoon ground black pepper to the ingredients before whisking.

Alternatively add 2 teaspoons crushed cumin seeds before whisking and serve with finely chopped mint or green coriander.

KADHO

This is a milk drink that is richly flavoured with ingredients such as saffron and nuts. This is normally served on special occasions, and in small amounts, because it is so rich.

Cooking and preparation time: 30 minutes   *Serves:* 6

500ml (1 pt) milk
2 tbsp sweetened condensed milk
115g (4 oz) evaporated milk
¼ tsp ground nutmeg
1 tsp ground cardamom
4 strands saffron
handful of almonds and pistachios, coarsely chopped

1. Mix all the ingredients together in a saucepan, bring to the boil and simmer for 30 minutes.

KESAR DOODH

Again, this is milk flavoured with saffron but it is not as rich as the Kadho. Serve as a night-time drink.

Cooking and preparation time: 15 minutes   *Serves:* 6

500ml (1 pt) milk
3 strands saffron
3 cloves
3 black peppercorns
2.5cm (1 in) cinnamon stick
2 cardamom pods
handful of almonds and pistachios, coarsely chopped
sugar to taste

1. Mix all the ingredients in a saucepan, bring to the boil and simmer for 12 minutes. Strain off whole spices and serve.

CHAI

This is a tea that is made in a simple way but tastes quite different from the 'English brew'! Serve at any time of day, although it is especially nice at breakfast with parathas or puris.

Cooking and preparation time: 15 minutes   *Serves:* 4–6

500ml (1 pt) milk
250ml (¼ pt) water
3–4 tea bags *or* 1 tbsp loose black tea
sugar to taste

1. Put all the ingredients in a saucepan, bring to the boil and then simmer on a low heat for 15 minutes.
2. Strain before serving.

MASALA CHAI

This again is made with very simple ingredients, but the spices give this tea a rich and distinctive flavour. This is especially warming on a cold winter day or last thing at night.

Cooking and preparation time: 25 minutes   *Serves:* 4–6

500ml (1 pt) milk
250ml (½ pt) water
3–4 tea bags *or* 1 tbsp loose black tea
1 tsp ginger powder
3 cloves
3 black peppercorns
2.5cm (1 in) cinnamon stick
2 cardamom pods
sugar to taste

1. Mix all the ingredients in a saucepan, bring to the boil and then simmer on a low heat for 20 minutes.
2. Strain the tea before serving.

RAAB

This drink is made from millet flour and spices. Serve hot, either in a mug or a soup bowl. It is very comforting when you have a cold!

Cooking and preparation time: 25 minutes   *Serves:* 6

25g (1 oz) butter or margarine
2 × 2.5cm (1 in) cinnamon sticks
4 cloves
4 black peppercorns
2 tbsp millet powder
50g (2 oz) brown sugar
½ tsp ginger powder
500ml (1 pt) water (or more if required)

1. Melt the butter or margarine in a saucepan and fry the whole spices for 2 minutes.
2. Add the millet flour and fry until it turns brown.
3. Next, add the rest of the ingredients and stir continuously until the mixture boils. Lower the heat and simmer for 20 minutes.

GUJARATI-STYLE TEA

Feel the warm glow down your throat as you sip this delicious warming tea on a cold winter's day. The Tea Masala is optional but it is well worth trying (see opposite). This tea can also be used to help soothe the throat when you are suffering from a cold.

Cooking and preparation time: 6–7 minutes   *Serves:* 2

420ml (15 fl oz) water
1cm (½ in) root ginger, grated
4 tsp granulated sugar
5–6 mint leaves
¼ tsp tea masala (see opposite) – optional
2 tsp tea leaves (any brand)
280ml (½ pt) full fat milk

1. Boil the water with the grated ginger in a small saucepan for 1 minute. Add the sugar, mint, tea masala and the tea leaves.
2. Boil for another minute. Now add the milk and bring to the boil. Simmer for 1 minute then strain into tea cups and serve.

UKARO

This hot spicy milk is a warming drink, best drunk at bedtime. Do watch over this as it has a tendency to boil over.

Cooking and preparation time: 7–12 minutes   *Serves:* 2

280ml (½ pt) water
2.5cm (1 in) root ginger, grated
3–4 mint leaves – optional
¼ tsp tea masala (see below)
4 tsp granulated sugar
570ml (1 pt) full fat milk

1. Put the water and grated ginger together in a milk pan and bring to the boil. Simmer for 1 minute, then add the mint leaves, tea masala and the sugar. Simmer for a further minute.
2. Now add the milk and bring back to the boil. Simmer for 1 more minute and strain into 2 tea cups.

TEA MASALA

You will need a coffee grinder for this recipe.

Preparation time: 5 minutes

115g (4 oz) white peppercorns
90g (3 oz) dried root ginger
60g (2 oz) cinnamon stick
28g (1 oz) cardamom seeds
25 cloves

1. Grind all the ingredients together in a coffee grinder and store in an airtight container. Tea masala will keep indefinitely if stored in this way.

Glossary of Ingredients and Spices

It is always cheaper to buy spices in larger packs rather than in small 55g (2 oz) cartons. Most Indian spices are cheaper at Indian grocery shops and, if you know the Indian names, it makes it that much easier.

Indian	English	Notes
Adrak (also **Adhrak, Adhu**, and **Adu**)	Ginger	A reddish-brown coloured root which has a very distinctive flavour, ginger is very commonly used in many Asian countries. It is regarded as a warming spice and is therefore used for medicinal purposes as well as for flavouring foods. It is available in fresh and powder form, and as a paste in jars. To use fresh ginger, remove the skin of the root, and then chop finely. In powdered form, the root is first dried and then ground. *Recommendation:* use fresh according to recipe.
Ajma	Carom or Celery seeds	Used in foods difficult to digest as it is believed to help digestion. Can be hot to taste if eaten raw.

Amli (also **Ambli**)	Tamarind	Usually dried, it is the very sour fruit of the tamarind tree, more commonly available in Britain in a block all stuck together. To use, break some off and soak in hot water for 10 minutes, then sieve through a wire mesh, extracting as much juice as possible. This juice is used to give a tangy flavour to some of the dishes.
Anardana	Pomegranate seeds	
Atta	Chapatti flour	Made from ground wheat.
Badam	Almonds	To loosen the skin of almonds for peeling, steep them in hot water for 10 minutes.
Besan (or **Chana na loth**)	Gram flour	A flour made from chick peas, described as gram flour on the packaging.
Bindi (also **Bhindi**)	Okra or ladies' fingers	A vegetable, green in colour, and available fresh and tinned. *Recommendation:* best used fresh; dry it very well after washing.
Chana (also **White chana** and **Chite chole**)	Chick peas	These are rich in iron and there are several ways of cooking them. It is usually necessary to soak them overnight. A pressure cooker is very useful when cooking whole pulses. Flour made from chick peas is often called gram flour or besan. It forms the basis of many Indian snacks.
Chana dhal	Split pulses	

Chapatti flour	Flour	A flour made from ground wheat, suitable for making chapattis, puris and parathas
Dahi	Natural yoghurt	Can be bought but is very easy to make at home (see page 245).
Dalchini (also **Tuj** and **Taj**)	Cinnamon stick	Cinnamon is available in two forms: cinnamon stick which is the dried bark of the Asiatic shrub, broken into smaller pieces; and the powdered form, which can be used instead of the stick. It is a strong spice used in powdered form in many sweet dishes. The stick cinnamon is more commonly used in curries and is discarded before serving.
Dhal (also **Daal, Dal** and **Dall**)	Split, shiny lentils	Dhal is also the name of a dish made with lentils.
Dhania (also **Dhana, Dhanyia** and **Dhunia**)	Coriander	Coriander is available in three forms. The fresh leaf of this green herb (dhunia) is used for flavouring and for garnishing most Indian dishes. It is very similar to fresh parsley which can be used for garnishing instead. Ground coriander (dhana) is one spice that can be used in larger quantities than any other. It has a subtle flavour and is used for thickening sauces. Coriander seeds are also used for flavouring. *Recommendation:* use fresh for garnish and in powder form for sauces.
Dhokra	Flour	Mixture of ground rice and ground chana dhal available from most Indian grocery shops.

Elchi (also **Alchee, Elichi**, and **Lachi**)	Cardamom	Used in many sweet and savoury dishes alike, cardamom is a dried fruit with very aromatic seeds. Several of the seeds are enclosed together in a light green or creamish-white coloured pod. Cardamom pods can be used whole or the seeds can be removed and then used in curries, while the seeds are crushed and added to sweet dishes. The seeds are also chewed after a meal to aid digestion.
Garam Masala	Literally means ' hot spices'.	It is a mixture of several spices in varying proportions. Garam masala adds a distinctive Oriental flavour to a dish. It is a combination of coriander powder, cumin powder, black peppercorns, ginger powder, cinnamon powder, pimento, cardamom powder, ground bay leaves, ground cloves and nutmeg. For a recipe see page 247. It is available from Asian shops and supermarkets.
Ghee	Clarified butter	Readily available in most Indian grocery shops but can be made quite easily at home. For instructions see page 246. *Recommendation:* make your own.
Goovar	Indian bean	Green in colour, it is flat and pointed at one end.
Gor	Jaggery	Sugar in the most unrefined state. It is sold in solid blocks and is readily available in most Indian grocery shops. If gor is not available it can be substituted with dark brown sugar.

Guaer	A vegetable	An uncommon vegetable which is available from most Indian shops and has to be bought fresh.
Gulab jamboo flour	Flour mix	A ready-made flour mix to make jamboos and sold under this name.
Haldi	Turmeric	A root similar to ginger. It is yellow in colour and can be used fresh if peeled and minced before use. It is commonly used in powder form and is available in most Indian grocery shops. Haldi is also said to be good for the skin. For a very economical face mask, mix together 1 tablespoon of thick cream, 1 teaspoon of ground haldi and a few drops of lemon juice. Indians who have little money for expensive medicines sometimes rub haldi on cuts as it has antiseptic properties. *Recommendation:* in cooking use the powder.
Hing	Asafoetida	A strong spice which should be used in small quantities, hing is a gum resin which is available either in gum or powder form. It has a very strong smell, and is mainly used for flavouring. It also aids digestion. It is available in most Indian shops but is not generally found in supermarkets. Some of the curries in this book use hing, but if it is not available, then the curry can be cooked without it. The fragrance of the curry will be less strong but only a small difference in taste is apparent.

Jaiphal (also **Jaifal** and **Jaifar**)	Nutmeg	Nutmeg, a digestive spice used in many savoury and sweet dishes and cordials, is the very hard, aromatic seed of a tree. The seeds are ground. Most supermarkets stock nutmeg, either whole or powdered. The whole nutmeg often has the best flavour and aroma. It can be grated straight into the dish. *Recommendation:* best used freshly ground.
Jeera	Cumin	A spice with a wonderful flavour which shows its full potential in yoghurt dishes. Available in seed or powder form, cumin is the dried fruit of an umbelliferous plant, which is used for flavouring. It is widely used in curries and pickles. *Recommendation:* use both types according to recipe.
Juwar flour	Flour	Flour made from ground barley.
Kadu	A vegetable	An uncommon vegetable which is available from most Indian shops and has to be bought fresh. The closest approximation is marrow, which can be used instead.
Kala Mari (also **Kali mirch sabat** and **Marri**)	Black peppercorns	A hot spice widely used in Indian cookery, black peppercorns are mainly used in savoury snacks and biryanis. It is the fruit of a plant and is easily obtainable in most supermarkets. Used whole in curries it is discarded before serving. Ground peppercorn is used in spicy snacks that are often sold in many Indian grocery shops, and used in raitas and pickles.

Karela	A vegetable	A green vegetable which looks like a cucumber with lots of bumps, pointed at both ends. It has a bitter taste.
Kessar (also **Kesar**)	Saffron	Dried stigmas of the crocus flower, they appear red/orange in colour and are very expensive, although keep for years! This very expensive ingredient must be used in moderation. Mainly used in sweet dishes and biryanis. *Recommendation:* use sparingly.
Lapsi	Cracked wheat (bulgar)	
Lasan	Garlic	Strongly flavoured and easily grown in the garden in the summer months. The root is much stronger than the shoots, so when a mild garlic flavour is desired use the top of the plant. Garlic is said to have aphrodisiac properties! It is available fresh or can be bought as paste in jars or in powdered form. It is a very strong-smelling bulb, consisting of a number of small sections, known as cloves of garlic. To use fresh garlic, remove the skin from the clove, and chop finely. For the powdered form, the garlic is dried and then ground, or it can be purchased already powdered. *Recommendation:* use fresh for best flavours.
Lavang (also **Laving**)	Cloves	Cloves are the dried flower buds of a special Asiatic tree. They are used whole, for flavouring, in many curries. Widely used in sweet and savoury dishes, they have antiseptic properties and are

often chewed after meals to freshen the palate. *Recommendation:* use whole and ground for garam masala.

Limdi (also **Limbri**)	Curry leaves	These look like bay leaves and are available fresh or dried (although mainly dried). These grow on bushes and are used for their flavour. Whole leaves are used for garnish and young tender leaves are chosen for chutneys. Fresh leaves are sometimes available in Indian grocery shops but their flavour is nothing like that of freshly picked leaves.
Madras	Curry powder	Madras curry powder, very easily available from most supermarkets, is a mixture of cumin powder, chillies, turmeric powder, ground mustard seeds, ground poppy seeds, garlic powder, and ground fenugreek.
Mari	Peppercorns	Available white or black, whole or ground. *Recommendation:* use whole black corns.
Masala	Spices	A word given to the collective spices used in a dish.
Masoor	Whole lentils	These are flat and round in shape. They are often found in biriyani dishes, soups and stuffings. They have a high food value as they are rich in protein.
Methi	Fenugreek	Fenugreek seeds are very dark orange in colour and are often used to grow fresh fenugreek. Ground fenugreek is used in making various mixed spices and in chutneys and pickles. Fresh

fenugreek is a vegetable, sometimes cooked like spinach. It is a herb with a mildly bitter taste, but the seeds produced by the plant have a much stronger bitter taste and are generally used to make pickles and medicinal concoctions.

Mircha (also **Mirchi**)   Chillies

Can be green or red, whole or just seeds. They are very hot and should be used in small quantities. As a rule, the smaller the chilli, the hotter it is. Chillies should be finely chopped or minced before adding to a dish. After handling chillies it is very important to wash hands thoroughly as it is very easy to transfer the heat of the chillies to other parts of the body, such as the eyes. Red chillies can be bought in powder form from most Indian grocery shops. Fresh green chillies are used in many recipes and are available at most supermarkets. Both are used in most Indian dishes which give them their distinctive hot flavour. Chilli powder is often available in varying degrees of hotness. Use milder forms of chilli powder initially. After some time, when you really want to try extra hot dishes, then either use slightly larger quantities of mild chilli powder, or buy a hotter variety.

Moong   Mung beans

These small, green beans are very popular. All Indian homes would have them. They are an excellent stand-by in the store cupboard. They can also be sprouted for use in salads.

Pouwa	Flaked rice	Available from most Asian shops and supermarkets.
Rai	Mustard seeds	Used for its pungent flavour, the seed is black or white and perfectly round. It can also be grown on the kitchen window sill for use in salads. The seeds from the pods of the yellow flowers are used for flavouring curries, and the powdered form is used for pickles. Both varieties of rai are available from most Asian shops or large supermarkets. Sometimes health food shops also sell rai. *Recommendation:* use whole black seeds.
Saragvo singh	A vegetable	Known as *drumsticks* in English. Green in colour, long (with ridges running down lengthwise) and pointed at both ends.
Soonf (or **Variari**)	Fennel seeds	Fennel seeds, like cumin, are also a dried fruit. They are used in some recipes and for making tea. Fennel seeds, light green in colour, have a very mild bitter taste. They are also often eaten raw.
Soy	Soy sauce	Soy sauce, an extract of soya beans, is not commonly used in India. Elsewhere, however, many Indian homes use it for cooking curries.
Taj	Cinnamon	See Dalchini.
Tandoori masala	A spice mix	Red in colour, tandoori masala is a combination of salt, coriander, cardamom powder, cinnamon powder, black peppercorns, cumin powder, ground cloves, chilli powder, ground bay leaves,

		mace, nutmeg, fenugreek powder, garlic powder and ginger powder. It is easily available in most large supermarkets.
Tikka (powder)	Mix of ground spices	A ready-made mix of spices, yellow in colour, available in large supermarkets.
Tindora	A vegetable	Uncommon, but available from Asian shops. It tastes like courgettes or cucumber and has to be bought fresh.
Toor (also **Toovar** or **Har har di dahl**)	Pigeon peas	These can be cooked whole but would require overnight soaking. Split pigeon peas, more commonly known as toor dhal, are used to make Dhal and Sambhar. It is very easy to mistake split chick peas (chana dhal) for split pigeon peas (toor dhal). The toor dhal is oily in appearance and slightly bigger than chana dhal.
Turmeric (powder)	Ground spice	Turmeric powder is the powdered form of the stem of a plant. It is bright yellow in colour and is widely available.
Urid (Also **Urad** or **Mahan di dahl**)	Black matape beans	Whole urid are black but they are rarely used whole, more commonly being de-husked and split or ground into flour. In the presence of water, urid flour becomes very sticky and it is this characteristic which makes it ideal for making poppadums.
Valor (also **Vallour**)	A type of bean	A rather uncommon vegetable, valor is available from most Indian shops, and has to be bought fresh.
Vermicelli	Pasta	Pasta in the form of fine tubes.